THE JOE E. BROWN FILMS

James L. Neibaur

The Joe E. Brown Films
By James L. Neibaur
Copyright © 2021 James L. Neibaur
No part of this book may be reproduced in any form or by any means, electronic, mechanical, digital, photocopying, or recording, except for inclusion of a review, without permission in writing from the publisher or Author.

No copyright is claimed for the photos within this book. They are used for the purposes of publicity only.

 Published in the USA by:
BearManor Media
1317 Edgewater Dr #110
Orlando, FL 32804
www.bearmanormedia.com

Perfect ISBN 978-1-62933-738-8
Case ISBN 978-1-62933-739-5
BearManor Media, Orlando, Florida
Printed in the United States of America
Book design by Robbie Adkins, www.adkinsconsult.com

Table of Contents

ACKNOWLEDGEMENTS v
DEDICATION vi
INTRODUCTION vii
JOE E BROWN: THE EARLY YEARS 1
THE EARLY SOUND MUSICALS 4
TOP SPEED 11
MAYBE IT'S LOVE 17
GOING WILD 24
SIT TIGHT. 30
BROADMINDED 35
LOCAL BOY MAKES GOOD 40
FIREMAN SAVE MY CHILD 47
THE TENDERFOOT 53
YOU SAID A MOUTHFUL 60
ELMER THE GREAT 66
SON OF A SAILOR 71
A VERY HONORABLE GUY 77
CIRCUS CLOWN 82
6 DAY BIKE RIDER 88
ALIBI IKE 95
BRIGHT LIGHTS 103
A MIDSUMMER NIGHT'S DREAM 111
SONS O' GUNS 118
EARTHWORM TRACTORS 124
POLO JOE 132
WHEN'S YOUR BIRTHDAY 137
RIDING ON AIR 143
FIT FOR A KING 151
WIDE OPEN FACES 156
THE GLADIATOR 161
FLIRTING WITH FATE 167

$1000 A TOUCHDOWN 172
BEWARE SPOOKS! 178
SO YOU WON'T TALK 183
SHUT MY BIG MOUTH 188
JOAN OF OZARK 194
THE DARING YOUNG MAN 200
CHATTERBOX. 206
CASANOVA IN BURLESQUE 211
PIN UP GIRL. 216
THE TENDER YEARS 223
SOME LIKE IT HOT AND THE LATER YEARS 228
BIBILOGRAPHY 235
INDEX 238

ACKNOWLEDGMENTS

As always, my first note of special thanks is for my assistant Katie Carter, who has lived every book with me for several years now, and makes each project better with her insights, and her uncanny ability to catch every one of my many typos.

Special thanks also to Richard Finnegan who kindly provided several beautiful photos to illustrate this book.

Special thanks to my friend, filmmaker John Gallagher, who freely shared his materials and interviews with me as he has on many of my projects. Sadly, John passed away while I was working on this project. I will miss his support and friendship forever.

And a shout out to childhood friend Peter Jackel who hurried over to my house with a DVD of *Son of a Sailor* when my disc turned out to be damaged.

Thanks also to the following:

Terri Lynch, Allie Schulz, Ted Okuda, Gary Schneeberger, Phil Hall, Kelly Parmelee, Wes Gehring, Leonard Maltin, Turner Classic Movies, Karen Zuehlke, Dave Lord Heath, and to the memory of my late son Max Neibaur, who will forever inspire everything I do.

DEDICATION:

For my new friend Marita Lynch, born November, 2020 just as I completed work on this project.

INTRODUCTION

For those whose only real knowledge of Joe E. Brown's work is his delightfully eccentric turn as Osgood Fielding in Billy Wilder's *Some Like it Hot* (1959), it may come as a surprise that he was the top drawing movie comedian of the 1930s. It wasn't Laurel and Hardy, The Marx Brothers, or W.C. Fields, it was Joe E. Brown. Brown was among the top ten box office stars in 1932, 1935, and 1936, which was the year when he reached his highest position of number five.

Joe E. Brown's career trajectory was decidedly unfortunate. Having been a circus performer, Joe also worked in vaudeville and in Broadway revues before he entered movies in the late 1920s. By the end of that decade he became a hit with the early color musical *On With The Show* (1929). Signed by Warner Brothers, Brown embarked on a series of starring comedies beginning in 1930 where he played everything from an earnest, loveable everyman, to a comically lofty braggart. His films delighted all ages and were a huge success at the box office. But a bad decision disrupted that momentum.

Brown always regretted the fact that he left Warner Brothers at the height of his fame in 1936 and began appearing in films for independent producer David Loew. His resulting films during the late 1930s were low budget B movies, and weren't the same level of quality as his Warner Brothers releases. Brown was still popular with audiences, but not as popular as his Warner Brothers releases had been, and exhibitor reports indicate that moviegoers did often notice the dip in quality. These later films also suffered from budgetary limitations as the Warner Brothers sets and locations were much more opulent than the lower cost features Brown made for Lowe.

By the end of the 1930s, Joe E. Brown's film career was relegated to B movies, which he continued to appear in for Columbia and Republic studios, save for supporting roles. He was an active entertainer of the troops during World War 2, especially after his son was killed in action in 1942. Thus, during the 1940s, his filming activities were decelerated.   Then in 1951, Joe E. Brown once again appeared in a film, as Cap'n Andy in *Show Boat*. It was one of only three movie appearances Brown made in the 1950s, the others being a small part in *Around The World in 80 Days* (1956) and his beloved performance in *Some Like it Hot*. Joe was one of many star cameos in Stanley Kubrick's epic *It's a Mad Mad Mad Mad World* (1963) and had a role the following year in *The Comedy of Terrors*, which was his last film appearance. He also did a lot of TV work during the 1950s, making his last television appearance also in 1964. Joe died in 1973 after being ill for some time.

In this study, Joe E. Brown's movies will be examined film by film, from his first 1930 starring comedy vehicle *Top Speed* through *The Tender Years*. A concluding chapter will look at his few film appearances after that, including *Some Like it Hot*, and his TV work. His presentation, how his athletic prowess informed his characters, the depth of skill he had as an actor, and his career trajectory will all be discussed. Despite his massive stardom during the first half of the 1930s, and his living into the 1970s, his impact did not last over time and generations, and if modern day audiences know him at all, it is for his appearance in *Some Like it Hot*. This book will make a case for Joe E. Brown's continued significance as a film comedian in the 21st century.

JOE E. BROWN: THE EARLY YEARS

Joseph Evan Brown was born July 28, 1891 in Holgate, Ohio. Joe would often joke that he was probably the only child to run away and join the circus with his parents' permission as Joe's large family needed the money he would earn while performing. Joe joined a group of circus tumblers, the Five Marvelous Ashtons, and toured the country, with the arrangement that his family would receive $1.50 per week (the equivalent of roughly $45.00 per week in the 2020s) while Joe's expenses would be covered by the circus.

Young Joe was very thin and a bit frail, but had great agility and a natural athletic ability. As a result, Joe fit in well with the acrobatic act, despite getting banged up quite a bit as he learned his moves; injuries that would continue to plague him well into adulthood. The Ashtons did a great deal of traveling, allowing Joe a real education as he experienced different audiences in a variety of cities throughout the nation. Some of the things he witnessed forced Joe to grow up very quickly. For instance, the Ashtons managed to be in the San Francisco area when the earthquake hit in 1906. Witnessing some of the atrocities of this event stayed with Joe for the rest of his life.

Returning to Ohio, Joe's natural athleticism found him joining the local semi-pro baseball team. His skills were so good, he was offered a position with the minor league division of the New York Yankees, but he turned it down to return to show business. However, he never completely left baseball. The sport would continue to inform his work, and his son Joe L. would become a noteworthy baseball manager years later.

Things weren't always good in vaudeville for teenaged Joe. He felt lonely and unhappy being away from his family during the Christmas season, and at one point during a botched routine he broke his leg on stage. One of the head members of the vaudeville troop, Frank Prevost, took Joe in. Prevost and his wife took care of Joe while he healed, and during his convalescence, Joe kept his spirits up joking with the Prevosts, keeping things light and amusing as his leg healed. Frank encouraged the naturally funny young man to add comedy to his act, and Joe fortunately accepted this advice.

Prevost and Brown put together an acrobatic comedy act and toured the vaudeville circuit throughout the nation, honing their routines as they went. They gradually became more and more popular and secured better bookings. It was during these tours that, in 1914, Joe met Kathryn McGraw, who became his wife the following year (they would stay married until Joe's death in 1973). Their first child, Donald, was born on Christmas day in 1916. In September of 1918, his son, Joe L. was born. The Browns would later adopt two daughters in the 1930s.

Frank Prevost was much older than Joe, and the time came for him to retire, but he encouraged Joe to continue as a single. Joe played the vaudeville circuit as a solo performer, and also played Burlesque during the 1918-1919 season. A big break came when he joined the show *Jim Jam Jems* in 1920 which also featured Harry Langdon. Langdon was performing his skit "Johnny's New Car," which he'd been honing on the vaudeville circuit for years. Langdon would later be one of the most creative silent screen comedians in film history and Joe respected the seasoned performer greatly. He would often watch Langdon's act from the wings and try to learn from the performer, who had an innate sense of timing that fascinated the younger comedian. Throughout the 1920s, Joe E. Brown would appear successfully in several Broadway shows, but never completely lost his love of baseball. He would even practice with professional teams at their Spring Training sessions during the 1920s.

Opportunities for Joe E. Brown to appear in movies came as early as 1928 at the closing of the silent era. None of these early movies showcased him at any level, and none are significant to his screen career. Perhaps his best during this period is *The Circus Kid* (1928). Joe's co-star was Frankie Darro who shared Joe's circus background, so they worked especially well together and responded effectively to the narrative's background. The film was generally a dramatic one;

Joe's character even dies at the end; but it was a hit and Joe received some recognition as an actor by moviegoers and critics.

In 1929 when the talking picture revolution happened Joe E. Brown left the small studios like FBO and Tiffany where he had been appearing in films, and signed with Warner Brothers. At first he was comic relief in some Technicolor musical features, but eventually emerged as one of the studio's biggest stars, and a top comedy attraction.

THE EARLY SOUND MUSICALS

First National Pictures was purchased by Warner Brothers in 1928 and from that point, all First National productions were released through Warner. Joe E. Brown's first appearance after signing with Warner Brothers was in the First National Pictures musical *On With The Show* (1929), which was based on the stage show *Shoestring*. Several popular songs, including "Am I Blue"(performed by Ethel Waters) were featured, and the movie starred Arthur Lake (later the movies' Dagwood Bumstead in Columbia's *Blondie* series) and Betty Compson. A largely dramatic film, Joe provides random comic relief in his role. The film was shot in two-strip Technicolor, a real innovation at the time being that it was also an early sound film, but, at the time of this writing, no color print of the film has survived over time.

On With The Show remains historically interesting as late as the 21st century due to its being an early example of the whole "putting on a show" concept, with creditors hovering about and threatening to close down the entire enterprise if they are not paid for their wares (scenery and costumes bought on credit against the show's grosses). The musical numbers are fun, and there are vignettes involving the various actors and performers that show different levels of conflict and romance.

Joe E. Brown and Arthur Lake have a rivalry throughout the film, with Lake complaining that Joe enters the stage too soon and "ruins all my love scenes." Joe responds, "I walk on before the audience walks out!" The press noticed the performances of both men, stating: "Joe E. Brown with his assortment of colored vests, and Arthur Lake, the popular juvenile, take care of the comedy and make a good job of it. Brown, in particular, is one of those natural comedians, who just can't behave, which makes things delightfully pleasant for audiences."[1]

---
1 "On With The Show" at Carolina Tomorrow. *Greenville News* July 28, 1929.

Ad for On With The Show

The next movie release in which Joe E. Brown is featured, *Painted Faces*, was actually a tardily released production from the low budget Tiffany studios. When compared to the more handsomely mounted *On With The Show*, the low budget trappings of *Painted Faces* are quite evident. It has some minor interest in that it is a serious drama where Joe plays Beppo, a circus clown who ends

Newspaper ad for Painted Faces

up on the jury for a trial regarding a vaudevillian who is murdered backstage. Beppo is the one holdout on the jury, believing the accused is innocent, and passionately trying to convince the others. It is interesting in that it shows Brown's innate talent as an actor, which would become more evident as his screen career developed.

Brown next appeared in *Sally* (1929), based on the musical comedy produced by Florenz Ziegfeld with a book by Guy Bolton and music by Jerome Kern. *Sally* is noted as being the film debut of stage star Marilyn Miller, who only appeared in four features before returning to the stage in 1931. She had a tragic life, dying at only 37 in 1936, so *Sally* has some significance as being one of the few existing films to feature her (the most noted might be *Her Majesty Love* (1931), and that's because it also features W.C. Fields). Marilyn Miller had played the lead in the Broadway production, so in order to secure her services for the movie, Warner Brothers paid her $1000 per hour, resulting in a total of $100,000. *Sally* was also filmed in two-strip Technicolor. Just like *On With The Show*, the color footage of *Sally* was unavailable until a color portion of the *Wild Rose* musical number was found in the 1990s and restored to the existing print.

Ad for Sally *which featured Broadway star Marilyn Miller*

In *Sally*, Joe E. Brown plays a deposed Grand Duke, who still holds the title but none of the associated benefits. Penniless, he tries to maintain some status in society circles. It is sort of a comic sub-plot tangential to the central narrative with Marilyn Miller playing the title character, but Joe does get to perform a delightful dance number with Miller, one of the highlights of the film. He also does a fun slapstick ladder bit with Jack Duffy.

Ad for Song of the West

An article in *The Oakland Tribune* discussed how director J. Francis Dillon worked out a short bit with Joe E. Brown:

The temperature outside the studio was close to a hundred and Dillon had been working since early morning, but he had the appearance of a gentleman who had just emerged from his tub; and his disposition was cooled to the same degree. He was going over a scene with Joe E. Brown (had Marilyn Miller been working,

Newspaper ad for Hold Everything

by the way, the studio would have been cleared of onlookers for Miss Miller has ideas on that matter), and the business of the scene was being discussed calmly and dispassionately. Twice Brown saluted the court without getting Dillon's Idea. They talked it over quietly and Dillon patiently demonstrated what he wanted. Brown saw the point, did the job and in a jiffy the scene was recorded.[2]

Sally was out of circulation for over 60 years, first becoming available for revival screenings in 1990. It is perhaps best known for its song, "Look For The Silver Lining." Along with Brown, former Keystone star Ford Sterling provides comic relief, and managed to generate the lion's share of comments from the critics.

Joe E. Brown had a bit more to do in his next movie appearance, *Song of the West* (1930), an operetta. Another two-strip Technicolor production, this one is noteworthy as the first all-talking feature to be filmed entirely outdoors. It was a more serious story with Brown providing comedy relief. However, he dies at the end, the result of a shootout. *Song of the West* is considered a lost film, with only the soundtrack discs and a color fragment of the film surviving at the time of this writing.

---

2   Soanes, Wood. Secrets of Directors Revealed. *Oakland Tribune*. August, 29, 1929

Perhaps *Hold Everything* (1930) could be considered the catalyst for Joe E. Brown's subsequent starring career as a comedian. Another two-strip Technicolor production, *Hold Everything* features Joe in a role performed by Bert Lahr on stage, as a third rate boxer who trains at the same camp where a top fighter works out. The film has romantic conflicts, fixed fights, and other formulaic situations that are bolstered by Joe's winning performance. *Hold Everything* was a huge hit, and among the top ten box office hits of 1930. The availability of this film has been limited since its release. Warner Brothers records indicate that the original negative was destroyed due to decomposition in December of 1948, but the sound discs survived. However, in the book *The Dawn of Technicolor* it is indicated that a black and white print of the film does exist in the UCLA archives.

It was Joe E. Brown's performance in *Hold Everything* that resulted in his being cast to star in *Top Speed*. Planned as another musical, most of the songs were cut from the film prior to release due to musicals suddenly becoming less popular with moviegoers during 1930. Thus, *Top Speed* was released as a straight comedy with Joe E. Brown in the starring role, and can be considered the true beginning of his motion picture career as a leading comedian.

TOP SPEED

Directed by Mervyn LeRoy
Screenplay by Harry Ruby, Bert Kalmar, Guy Bolton, Humphrey Pearson, Henry McCarty
Produced by Darryl F. Zanuck
Cinematography by Sidney Hickox
Film Editing by Harold Young

Songs:
As Long as I Have You
Music by Joseph A. Burke
Lyrics by Al Dubin

If You Were a Traveling Salesman and I Were a Chambermaid
Music by Joseph A. Burke
Lyrics by Al Dubin

Knock Knees
Music by Joseph A. Burke
Lyrics by Al Dubin

Looking for the Lovelight in the Dark
Music by Joseph A. Burke
Lyrics by Al Dubin

Cast:
Joe E. Brown, Bernice Claire, Jack Whiting, Frank McHugh, Laura Lee, Edmund Breese, Wade Boteler, Rita Flynn, Edwin Maxwell, Billy Bletcher, Al Hill, Cyril Ring, Gabby Hayes.

Released August 24, 1930
Running Time: 71 minutes
First National Pictures/Warner Brothers
Black and White

Joe E. Brown's popularity continued to increase with his appearances in the various musical comedies leading up to *Top Speed*, which was a comedy adapted to his talents for its screen version. The studio's promotion of the film often centered on Joe himself. Usually clad in wild checkered jackets and vests, the comedian's loud wardrobe was topic of an article used to promote *Top Speed*:

> Joe E. Brown, who is now playing in *Top Speed*, is noted for having the loudest wardrobe of any actor in Hollywood. The comedian has gathered the wardrobe during a period of years, and picked up some of his choicest possessions in smaller cities during tours on the road while he was still on the legitimate stage. "I have always worn loud clothes on the stage. But when I come to buy a wardrobe I find it tremendously hard to get noisy clothes, it is impossible at good stores, because they don't carry them, or won't show them if they have a few freaks in stock. However, you can often pick them up in out of the way places, or in cheap clothing stores in the poorer parts of town."[3]

In *Top Speed* Joe E. Brown plays bond clerk Elmer Peters, who, with his pal and workmate Gerald Brooks (Jack Whiting), get in trouble with the sheriff for fishing at a No Fishing area. They hide out at an expensive hotel where they meet two girls who were just involved in a car accident. Elmer falls for Babs (Laura Lee) while Jack becomes smitten with Virginia (Bernice Claire). Elmer and Gerald are mistaken for millionaires due to Elmer's boastful manner. Elmer's bragging causes Virginia to conclude that Gerald is a top speedboat racer, so when her father (Edwin Maxwell) needs someone to pilot his boat, she talks him into hiring her new beau. A rival (Edmund Breese) realizes Gerald is a phony and offers him a $30,000 bribe, which he accepts. However, when the race happens, he changes his mind, due to his love for Virginia, and wins the race.

Top Speed is something of a portent to Joe E. Brown's later films where he plays a confident braggart who must prove his boasts.

---

3   Joe E. Brown has the Loudest Wardrobe in Hollywood. *San Francisco Examiner.* September 7, 1930

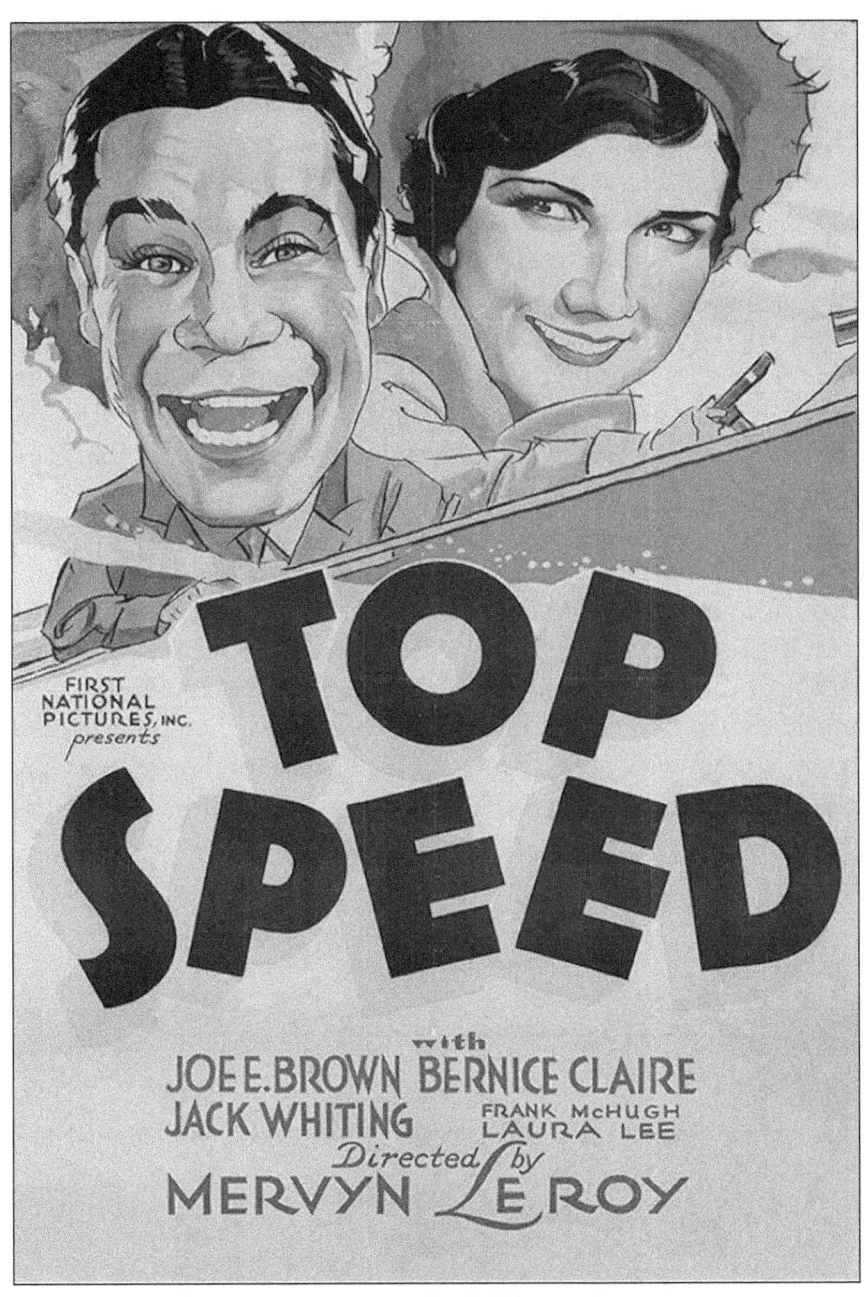

Ad for Top Speed

Some of his classic baseball comedies would use this as a basis a few years later. What is odd about *Top Speed* is that the existing print runs only 71 of its original 80 minutes due to several songs being removed before American distribution. As stated previously, musicals were losing their box office power, so Warner Brothers decided to release the film as a straight comedy. While retaining a few of the musical numbers, among the songs cut include "As Long as I Have You and You Have Me," "Goodness Gracious," "I'll Know and She'll Know," "Keep Your Undershirt On," "What Would I Care?" "Sweeter Than You," and "Reaching For the Moon." In the existing American release print, the music in the background will swell up during a scene, and then cut away before the song starts. In Europe, *Top Speed* was released with all of the songs intact. Only the Warner Brothers cut version still exists, but the complete soundtrack survives on discs at the UCLA television archive.

There are some interesting sociocultural aspects to *Top Speed* that make it more interesting in the 21st century. Not only is it significant in the context of Joe E. Brown's film career, it is also noteworthy as one of the few films in which Laura Lee appears. A stage actress in the 1920s, Lee made only 5 films before leaving show business, most of them with Joe E. Brown. Finally, the storyline where Gerald agrees to throw the race despite being a generally nice guy, has

Laura Lee and Joe E. Brown

a lot to do with the period in which this movie was produced. The Great Depression was such a time where the idea of turning down as much as $30,000 (equivalent to nearly half a million in 2020), would be nearly impossible for anyone, especially a small time working class sort. Thus, in the context of the narrative, the action is forgivable even before Gerald does the right thing and wins the race. It is also fun to see Warner Brothers stalwart Frank McHugh in an early role. McHugh would continue to enhance Warner movies with his winning performances throughout the 1930s.

For being an early talkie with somewhat primitive filmmaking technology, the speedboat scenes are effectively exciting. Sometimes the use of studio back projection is a bit lacking, but often the stock shots are seamlessly edited in with close-ups.

But most of the humorous highlights involve Joe E. Brown and Laura Lee. One such incident that could only be done in the pre-code era, is when two of Babs' friends are undressing to go to the pool, while Babs tries to conceal the fact that Elmer is hiding under the bed. Playful Elmer keeps trying to peek out from under the bed to catch a glimpse of the girls undressing. Realizing there is something under the bed, the girls become curious and Babs claims it is just a dog. Elmer, eating a banana, rubs the peel against one of the girls' hands when she reaches under the bed, after which she states, "yes it's a dog, it just licked my arm." The scene even has Laura Lee mimicking Joe's famous gap-mouthed yell.

During this period of film marketing, the promotional activities can often be quite interesting. In the case of *Top Speed*, a Warner Brothers theater in Memphis did the following, as reported in *Exhibitor's Herald World*:

> Six Austin automobiles, two bands, and a motorboat, all carrying banners, advertised First National's *Top Speed* at the Warner Brothers theater in Memphis. Tieup with a taxicab company gave the theater an additional bundle of promotion. Ninety cabs were stickered with this label: "This cab will take you at top speed to see *Top Speed* with Joe E. Brown." Through another tieup, 10,000 packages of Life Savers were enclosed in envelopes and distributed through the city. On the outside of the envelopes was the

following copy: "Warner Brothers theater. Have a Life Saver with you when you're going at top speed, and see *Top Speed* with Joe E. Brown. Starting Friday. Tops any comedy you've ever seen. Symbolizing the sport which plays an important part in the action of the film, a large motorboat was placed in the lobby. Window displays of sport wear were also obtained in some of the smartest shops in the city.[4]

Top Speed may seem a bit creaky as late as the 21st century, as many early talkies can be. But it is really a nice, compact entertainment vehicle that was a box office hit in its time, and continued to advance Joe E. Brown's film career. Essentially, at this early stage Joe considered himself a stage comedian who was doing movies, rather than a movie actor. Thus, the musical comedy vehicles that allowed him to bank off of his stage persona and expand it to the screen was an effort to promote subsequent theatrical work.

Joe E. Brown would have more to do in his next film, *Maybe It's Love*, which would be directed by the esteemed William Wellman. As he continued to make movies, Joe would evolve into an actor and expand upon his screen persona.

---

4   Bands, Motorboat And Tieups Promote Top Speed Picture. *Exhibitors Herald-World*. October 18, 1930.

MAYBE IT'S LOVE

Directed by William Wellman
Produced by Darryl F. Zanuck
Screenplay: Joseph Jackson based on the stories, "Footloose Widows" and "Maybe It's Love" by Darryl F. Zanuck (billed as Mark Canfield).
Cinematography: Robert Kurrle.
Film Editing: Edward M. McDermott.

Songs:
Maybe It's Love
Music by Archie Gottler and George W. Meyer
Lyrics by Sidney D. Mitchell

All American
Music by Archie Gottler and George W. Meyer
Lyrics by Sidney D. Mitchell

Keep It Up for Upton
Music by Archie Gottler and George W. Meyer
Lyrics by Sidney D. Mitchell

Cast:
Joe E. Brown, Joan Bennett, James Hall, Laura Lee, Sumner Getchell, George Irving, George Bickel, Russell Saunders, Stuart Erwin, Tim Moynihan, Bill Banker, Howard Harpster, Ray Montgomery, Otto Pommerening, Red Sleight, Kenneth Haycraft, George Gibson, Paul Scull, Dave O'Brien, W. K. Schoonover, Howard Jones, Fred Kohler, jr. Anders Randolf, Tom Hanlon, Fred Lee, Harry Strathy.

Released October 4, 1930
Running Time: 71 minutes.
Warner Bros./Vitaphone
Black and White
Alternate title: Eleven Men and a Girl

It is somewhat surprising that a director the caliber of William Wellman was responsible for the mildly amusing, but ultimately rather lackluster *Maybe It's Love*. It is sort of an aberration in the director's career, and one that rarely enjoys much discussion among his films.

Joe E. Brown plays Speed Hansen, a college football hero who schemes with his gal pal Nan (Joan Bennett) to entice top level college athletes to attend their university and play for their team. Nan flirts effectively, convincing a myriad of top college football stars that she is quite fond of them. They all take the bait, enroll in the University, and join the team. One special case is Tommy Nelson (James Hall), whose college exploits have been financed by his rich father (Anders Randolf). Dad has also bailed the entitled young man out of several jams. When arrangements are made for Tommy to attend a prestigious college, he too is sidetracked by Nan's advances and ends up "slumming" at her state university without his father's knowledge. This is a real boon for the football team as Tommy is a top-level athlete. Joining the football team as their star player, he enrolls under the name "Tommy Smith" to further keep his father from realizing where he's attending. Of course there comes a time when the men all get wise to Nan's shallow romantic promises, and threaten to not play, as she genuinely falls for Tommy. On top of this, Tommy's father discovers that his son is a student at the state college and threatens to pull him out of there at once. Speed has to kidnap Tommy's father and remain locked in a basement with him until the game is played. Of course it all works out in the end when the State team wins the big game, and Tommy's father accepts Nan.

The material here is amusing, but slight; an effective programmer but not worthy of a director the caliber of Wellman who had directed *Wings* (1927), the first film to win a Best Picture Oscar. This was his first film for Warner Brothers, and he was given a vehicle that was rejected by Michael Curtiz (another director too good for this material). Wellman would next helm the classic *Public Enemy*, one of the movies that helps define this era of his career. *Maybe It's Love* has been blissfully forgotten.

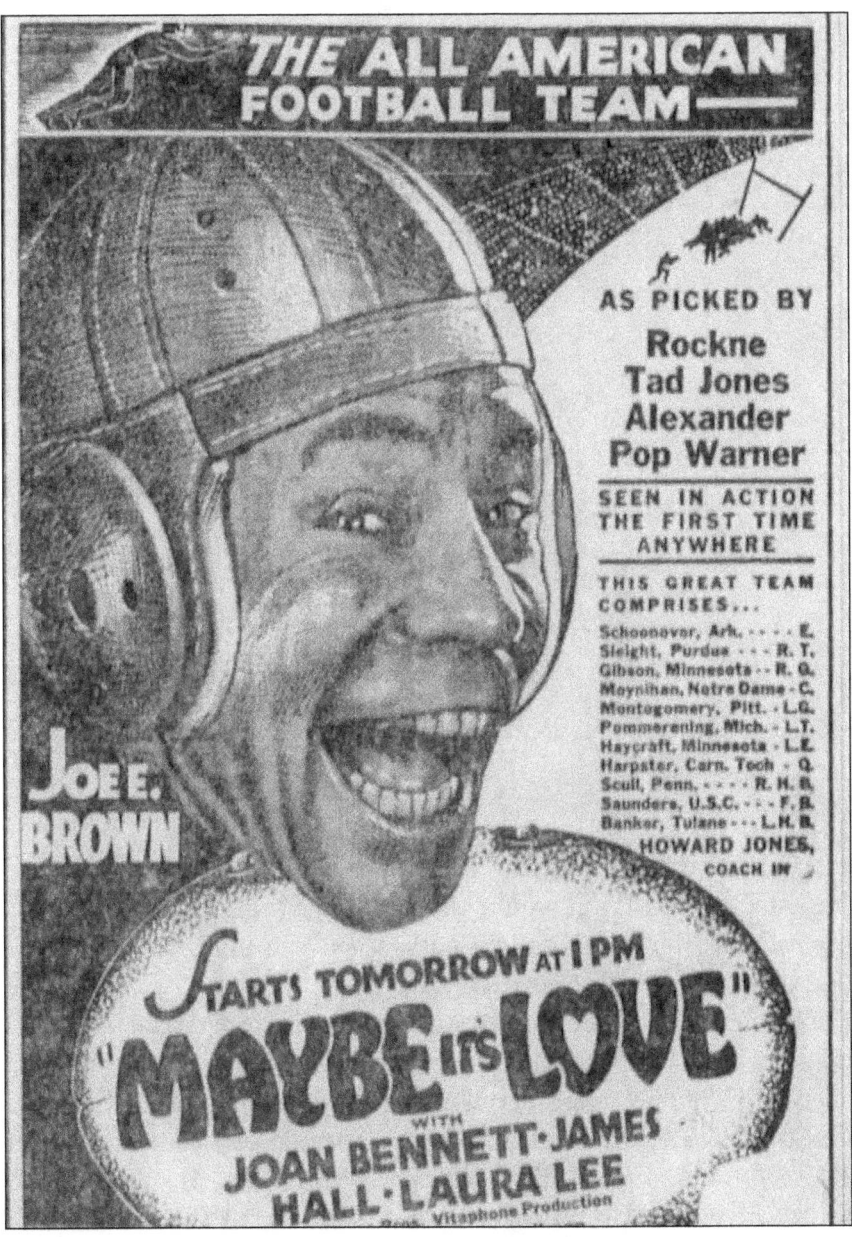

Newspaper ad for Maybe It's Love

As it stands, Joe E. Brown is the main attraction, along with an early appearance by strikingly pretty Joan Bennett. Brown continued to established a real niche by transitioning his comic character to movies, taking advantage of his big mouth with several

Joe E. Brown and Laura Lee

"waaaooo" howls emphasizing its imposing size. This was a part of Joe's stage work, and it would also become a very central part of his screen character. Joan Bennett's character Nan starts out as myopic and mousy, but both Speed and his girl Betty (Laura Lee) can see the beauty behind the surface and realize if she were fixed up she could be a real knockout.

Football movies were popular at this time, including the 1929 Fox film *Salute*, which also had been penned by production chief Daryl Zanuck under the pseudonym Mark Canfield. Subsequent football comedies in the 30s would include Bert Wheeler and Bob Woolsey in *Hold 'Em Jail* (RKO, 1932) and The Marx Brothers in *Horse Feathers* (Paramount, 1932). The football scenes are enjoyable and exciting, and the comic antics of Joe E. and Anders Randolf in attempting to climb boxes and watch the game thru a window while locked in the basement offer some good slapstick fun.

Randolf had done films with both Charley Chase and Laurel and Hardy by this time, and was no stranger to knockabout comedy. Randolf would appear in Joe's next feature, *Going Wild* due to his working so well with the comedian.

Laura Lee was a successful stage actress who made only five movies and then returned to stage work. Three of those films featured Joe E. Brown, including the previous *Top Speed*, and this one. She would also appear in his next, *Going Wild*.

The idea of using actual athletes in the role of the college football players was a neat touch, and likely helped the box office. It was stunt casting, to be sure, but it allowed the football scenes to be more realistic and exciting. Interestingly, one article on the film appeared to indicate that *Maybe It's Love* was the first, or one of the first, movies that revealed what went on in the locker room between halves.

> One of the features of a great football game that the throngs in the stadium never see or hear is revealed in *Maybe It's Love*, the Warner Brothers and Vitaphone picture of college life, in which Joan Bennett, Joe E. Brown, James Hall, Laura Lee and others appear. At the end of the first half, when the pigskin warriors trot off the gridiron to their dressing quarters, what goes on behind those closed doors? What does the fighting coach say? How do the players feel? This moment, never witnessed by the fans, provides one of the dramatic scenes of *Maybe It's Love*. Howard Jones, coach of the University of Southern California, enacts the role of the coach of the "All- American" football team in the picture. His characterization is based upon his years of coaching experience and what actually happens between halves of a big game"is photographed and recorded with accuracy.[5]

Joe E. Brown has more to do in *Maybe It's Love* than he had in *Top Speed*, and he makes the most of his scenes. He and Bennett seemed to get an equal amount of attention from the various

---

5   Dramatic Scenes of Football Shown On Screen. *Cincinnati Inquirer.* November 23, 1930

reviews, most of which were quite positive. Karl Krug in the *Pittsburgh Press* stated:

> A thoroughly enjoyable comedy ... a fast and spirited grid battle rolled together nicely by Mr. William Wellman, the director .... More than once Mr. Brown gracefully steps aside to let Miss Bennett, Mr. Hall and the gridiron heroes handle the picture by themselves and the film doesn't suffer. When hilarity is needed Mr. Brown can be depended upon to provide it ... It never takes itself seriously and doesn't expect movie audiences to take it seriously either. Last night at the Stanley the folks went after it in exactly the right spirit. Even Miss Bennett and Mr. Hall singing a love ballad at each other didn't throw a damper on the fun. *Maybe It's Love* waltzed right through to a well deserved hearty reception. Director Wellman has handled the football game with skill.[6]

Edwin Schallert of *The Los Angeles Times* seemed to enjoy the film also, and was pleased with Joe E. Brown and Joan Bennett, but not too impressed with the acting of the football stars:

> As actors, the all-Americans are excellent football players. They make their debut in *Maybe It's Love*, which Is showing at Warner's Hollywood Theater, and they do themselves credit in the gridiron scenes. They may also qualify as a glee club, though I have the faint suspicion that their voices are dubbed. Anyway, you may see Euss Saunders, Tom Moynihan, W. K. Schoonover, Bill Banker and others, besides Coach Howard Jones in the pigskin classic, which features Joe E. Brown, Joan Bennett and James Hall thespianically. Incidentally, one must credit Jones, as coach, with speaking his lines with genuine authority. *Maybe It's Love* will satisfy those who regard Joe Brown as a hilarious comedian, and who want to see the home team come up from behind and win. Brown is unquestionably uproarious, especially funny being his repeated crescendo shouting of "U-p-t-o-n." Joan Bennett is the charmer of the picture,

---

6   Krug, Karl. Maybe It's Love review. *The Pittsburgh Press*. October 17, 1930

and because of the dainty attractiveness of her personality, can almost make you believe that she would allure football heroes from all over the continent. Hall sings a song or two in this feature, as well as donning the headgear for the big game, and also making love to Miss Bennett. The story of *Maybe It's Love* is credited to Mark Canfield, and screen play and dialogue was devised by Joseph Jackson. William Wellman directed.[7]

In 1935, Warners released another movie with the title *Maybe It's Love*. It wasn't a remake, and had nothing to do with the 1930 feature. However, the similarity in titles is why TV prints of the Joe E. Brown film now have the title *Eleven Men and a Girl*.

Joe E. Brown was continuing to turn into a likeable comic presence and his movies were enjoying solid box office success. He next appeared in a supporting role for an independent production from Joseph Schenck for United Artists. *The Lottery Bride,* starring then newcomer Jeanette McDonald, was probably filmed before Joe began building his screen character at Warner Brothers. *The Lottery Bride* was released in November of 1930 at 80 minutes and featuring a color sequence. It was re-released in 1937 but at a truncated 67 minutes and missing its color footage. It was restored in 2011 by the George Eastman house.

Brown's next starring film would be *Going Wild*, which Warners used to continuing building his career and the popularity that was advancing and ensuring good box office.

---

7   Scallert, Edwin. Maybe It's Love review. *The Los Angeles Times*. October 20, 1930.

GOING WILD

Directed by William Seiter
Screenplay: Humphrey Pearson based on *The Aviator* by James Montgomery
Cinematography: Sol Polito
Film Editing: Peter Fritch

Song:
My Hero Mine
Music by Fred E. Ahlert
Lyrics by Roy Turk

Cast:
Joe E. Brown, Lawrence Gray, Ona Munson, Walter Pidgeon, Laura Lee, Frank McHugh, May Boley, Anders Randolf, Arthur Hoyt, Johnny Arthur, Fred Kelsey, Harvey Clark, Larry Banthim, Max Wagner, Allan Cavan, Larry Banthim, Floyd Shackelford, Richard Coleman, Hayes Robinson, Bill Elliot, Bess Flowers, Clifford Ingram, Florence Wix, Polly Ann Young, Hal Roberts, Birgil Owens, Matthew Jones, Henry Hall, Clifford Ingraham.

Released December 21, 1930
Running Time: 68 minutes.
First National Pictures/Warner Brothers
Black and White

Going Wild is the third movie in which Joe E. Brown starred that began as a musical but was edited down to remove the songs when test screenings continued to present a lack of interest in musicals. *Going Wild* is similar to the earlier *Top Speed* in that Joe E. Brown once again presents himself as something he is not, and circumstances force him to prove himself.

Daredevil Joe in Going Wild

This one has Joe as Rollo Smith who, with his buddy Jack Lane (Lawrence Gray) is on a train with no tickets or money. They try to generate cash to remain on the train by playing poker to win some funding, but when they lose the hand, they're kicked off the train at the next stop. As the train is coming to this stop, Rollo and Jack meet a writer named Robert Story whose best-selling book about aviation has worn him to a frazzle due to the otherwise private man being accosted by too much attention. As a result, he is now trying to avoid all publicity and the stress that goes with it. Mr. Story is not the dashing aviator his book would have one believe, but a small, jittery man who, at this point, just wants to be left alone. When Rollo and Jack are dropped off at the train's next stop, they are met by a massive fanfare for Robert Story, having expected the famous writer and aviator to disembark the train for an appearance. However, Story has decided not to leave the train. And, since nobody has ever seen the actual Story, Rollo pretends to be the author-aviator. As a result, he and Jack are treated like royalty. They get free rooms at the best hotel, never have to pay for their food, and are given a great deal of celebratory attention. However, Rollo is then asked to participate in an important air race against an actual pilot, the townspeople believing they can count on this famous aviator to win the race. However, Rollo has never even been on an airplane, much less flown one.

The removal of all songs except one tightens the pace of *Going Wild* to where it runs a brisk 68 minutes and maintains interest throughout. Perhaps the best of Joe E. Brown's films thus far, *Going Wild* benefits not only from the amusing characters and situations, but also a couple of especially funny set-pieces that add a slapstick element to the proceedings.

Joe E. Brown is quite amusing early in the film as Rollo and Jack loftily strut about as celebrities, enjoying free room and meals at a swank hotel. Rollo even gladly signs Robert Story's autograph when presented with the author's book by various fans. One especially amusing scene has a long line of attractive women in line to get their book autographed. Rollo signs Story's name, and also includes his hotel room number. This was comfortably allowed during the pre-code area, but the more restrictive production code that was enforced a few years later would likely have insisted it be jettisoned.

There is some level of specific romance added to the narrative. Despite his flirtatious actions during the autograph sessions, Rollo is mostly smitten with Peggy (Laura Lee) who owns the hotel with her drunken brother Ricky (Frank McHugh). Meanwhile Jack has fallen for Peggy's friend Ruth (Ona Munson).

When Rollo first discovers he is expected to pilot a plane for a big race, he practices in his room by balancing atop his upright bed and using a vacuum cleaner and other props in an attempt to simulate

Joe takes some chances in Going Wild

flight. An outrageously funny visual, it ends with everything crashing to the ground. Rollo wants to leave and avoid humiliation and danger, but Jack wants to stay and romance Ruth. Rollo attempts to sneak out down the fire escape with his suitcase, but is spotted by Peggy and rival aviator Ace Benton (Walter Pidgeon). Ace has Rollo pegged as a phony from the start, so Rollo puts his suitcase in a nearby tree, and comes down the fire escape insisting he was not ducking out, despite how it looks. His suitcase then falls on his head, so he yells up to Jack and tells him to stop goofing around. It is comically desperate, and it works.

Perhaps the biggest laughs come from the examination sequence when Rollo is tested by several doctors as to his fitness for aviation. Rollo is x-rayed and the machine starts on fire. He is put in a simulated aircraft that flips and flies rapidly as he wails in protest. This physical comedy suits Brown nicely and enhances the narrative without distracting from it. However, when the film was released, some articles claimed it was a bit too close to a scene in a recently released Bert Lahr movie. According to newspaper reports:

> The case history of Joe E Brown's hilarious medical examination scene in *Going Wild*, reveals that, while it is similar to Bert Lahr's plight in *Flying High*, it was not lifted from the George White Show, as had been hinted. A telegraphic inquiry to Humphrey Pearson and Henry McCarty, who did the screen story and the dialogue for *Going Wild*, brought back the response that while they had heard of the medical examination scene In *Flying High*, neither one of them had seen the show or read the script. They point out further that production was begun on *Going Wild* only three days after *Flying High* opened at the Apollo Theatre. New York. This medical examination scene, in which a. doctor loses a spoon within the cavernous depths of Joe E. Brown's a mouth as he says, "Ah," has been cited by reviewers as the one most hilarious sequences in any picture during the past year.[8]

More than one review of *Going Wild* pointed out how audiences shrieked with laughter during the examination scene, and the critics were fairly unanimous in considering *Going Wild* to be Joe E. Brown's best movie to date.

Once again, this movie was released in Europe with its musical numbers intact, while in America only the truncated version was released. And, as with many of the previous films that were later pared down, there is no complete print of *Going Wild* that survives. We only have the abridged version.

Filming completed in July of 1930, and at about the same time, cast member Anders Randolf died suddenly after an operation. Randolf had been especially memorable working with Joe E. Brown in *Maybe It's Love* and, as indicated in that chapter, had also appeared in comedies with Laurel and Hardy and Charley Chase. He was quite a noted actor in Hollywood, and his passing resulted in what has been described as a grand funeral. His widow and child moved back to their native Sweden after his death.

---

8   About Joe E. Brown and his Latest Film. *Brooklyn Times Union.* February 8, 1931.

Going Wild was not only Joe E. Brown's best film to date, it was also his biggest box office hit. This was mostly due to Joe himself, whose affable manner was connecting effectively with audiences who needed escapism at the outset of the Great Depression. Warner Brothers recognized the comedian's growing popularity, and the box office returns for *Going Wild*. Continuing to be among the most popular film performers in movies, Joe next began filming yet another musical comedy. And, once again, *Sit Tight* was also released without its musical numbers.

SIT TIGHT

Directed by Lloyd Bacon
Screenplay: William K. Wells, based on story by Rex Taylor
Cinematography: William Rees
Film Editing: James Gibbon

Song:
Face It with a Smile
Music by Abel Baer
Lyrics by L. Wolfe Gilbert

Cast:
Joe E. Brown, Winnie Lightner, Paul Gregory, Claudia Dell, Lotti Loder, Hobert Bosworth, Frank Hagney, Snitz Edwards, Maurice Black, Arthur Hoyt, Tom Ricketts, Heinie Conklin, Tom Kennedy, Richard Cramer, James Eagles, Kalla Pasha, Constantine Romanoff, Kewpie Morgan.

Released February 28, 1931
Running Time: 76 minutes.
Warner Brothers
Black and White

Sit Tight was another full-blown musical, and shot that way, but released with all but one of its musical numbers cut. Joe E. Brown benefits from being teamed with vaudeville and Broadway star Winnie Lightner, who had appeared with Joe in his early film *Hold Everything*. She only made about 14 films before leaving movies in 1934 and marrying director Roy Del Ruth.

Winnie runs a health club and Joe (called Jojo in the film) is a smitten employee who has a wrestling background. He and Winnie agree to train Tom (Paul Gregory) who plans to become a wrestler after a rift with his girlfriend, Sally (Claudia Dell). Tom has

Joe and Winnie Lightner

been working for Sally's father (Hobart Bosworth), and she cajoles her dad into promoting him to a more advanced position. But Tom wants to earn his way up, and not rely on benevolent charity, so he turns down the promotion. This upsets Sally and she asks her father to fire him. Because Tom is a good worker, the father doesn't want to fire him. However, Tom is angered by the situation and quits his job, which leads him to the wrestling idea and hooking up with Winnie and Jojo.

Sit Tight is perhaps the weakest of Joe E. Brown's early 1930s musicals that were recut to play as straight comedies. While generally pleasant, it is missing the upbeat, cheerful pace of *Going Wild*. The dialog is often amusing, especially the repartee between Brown

Joe and Winnie Lightner

and Winnie Lightner. Winnie is known for her quick quips and Joe keeps up with her quite handily. And both performers have ample charisma. But the sub-plot between Tom and his girl seems more like a distraction, even though it is central to the narrative.

There are some comic highlights. A chase through the cavernous health club, when a larger man (Frank Hagney) believes Joe has been flirting with his wife, allows director Lloyd Bacon to take advantage of the set, and create an effective succession of shots to best enhance the sequence. Joe's flirtatious reaction to pretty Lotti Loder is fun when she is shown to initially be amused by his manner, until he pats her knee. She then abruptly turns on Joe, and yells at him for "taking liberties."

Perhaps the strongest sequence has Joe taking part in a makeshift wrestling bout to kill time until Tom arrives to take on the champion. Joe is fighting a masked wrestler who, during the bout, has his mask removed and is revealed to be the irate husband who believed Joe was flirting with his wife. Joe fluctuates from determined confidence to base cowardice, while Brown's athletic prowess results in some good slapstick flips and falls in the ring. There are some standard gags (Joe discovering he is twisting his own foot, and later patting his opponent's back to trick him into thinking

Joe enters the wrestling ring against Frank Hagney in Sit Tight

he's won). But a dream sequence where Joe is knocked out during the wrestling bout, dreams he is watching Winnie dance as a harem girl, and wakes up kissing the referee (Tom Kennedy), isn't particularly funny and slows down the pace of the scene. Still, the wrestling match is well shot and well performed enough to be this film's highlight. Brown would revisit pro wrestling with a similar scene in his much later film *The Gladiator* (1938).

The championship bout in which Tom wrestles is supposed to be the climactic highlight, but since it is part of the romantic sub-plot and played more seriously, it comes off as less interesting than Joe's more comical bout. There is perhaps a historical-cultural interest in seeing how a professional wrestling match was performed back in 1931 (much more seriously than the "sports entertainment" style of more recent times). But after the wild slapstick of Joe's wrestling match, the film asks us to shift gears and respond to a wrestling bout that is to be taken seriously. Going from comedy to drama disrupts the flow of the film's structure. Cutaways to Joe and Winnie rooting for Tom help build up the scene's rhythm, but only slightly.

Critic Jack Grant's review in the *Motion Picture News* indicates that not only was *Sit Tight* well received, the climactic wrestling match was deemed an exciting finale:

If anything, a wrestling match is better thrill material on the screen than the more familiar prizefight finale. It has been nicely staged in this release and looks mighty real. Though the result may be pre-determined by any smart audience, there is no denying it packs a punch.

The same review also responded well to Joe E. Brown, stating:

The burlesque wrestling bout is unquestionably the picture's highlight. From the first flash of Brown's pan, the gang is with him. His style of comedy remains unique in films and the wrestling travesty will leave them howling. Few more hilarious sequences have ever been filmed.[9]

While *Sit Tight* does not hold up quite as well as other Joe E. Brown comedies, Jack Grant's review gives us an idea of how well it resonated at the time of its initial release. It was another box office hit for Joe E. Brown. One exhibitor happily stated: "It was twice as funny as his funniest. Everybody seeing the picture will like it. No disappointments, guaranteed."[10]

Sit Tight was so popular with moviegoers, it was moved to larger theaters when the smaller ones kept filling up where it was playing. But despite its popularity and box office strength, reports in the trades indicated that Joe E. Brown's contract may not be renewed because musicals were on the wane and his salary was also an issue. Of course, Warner Brothers did decide to renew his contract, and his popularity continued to grow to the point where he became one of the studio's most lucrative stars.

In March of 1931, Joe E. Brown began filming his next feature, *Broadminded*. This time it was not originally conceived as a musical, but was instead a comedy by Bert Kalmar and Harry Ruby penned exclusively for Joe. It features Bela Lugosi, whose career defining movie *Dracula* was making the rounds in theaters during filming. It also features Marjorie White, an actress who made a discernible impact with comedians before her tragic death. Unfortunately, it was an even weaker film than *Sit Tight*.

---

9   Grant, Jack. Sit Tight review. *Motion Picture News*. October 4, 1930.
10 The Barometer. *Motion Picture News*. June 2, 1931

BROADMINDED

Directed by Mervyn LeRoy
Screenplay: Bert Kalmar and Harry Ruby
Cinematography: Sid Hickox
Film Editing: Al Hall

Cast:
Joe E. Brown, Ona Munson, William Collier jr. Marjorie White, Holmes Herbert, Margaret Livingston, Thelma Todd, Bela Lugosi, Grayce Hampton, George Grandee, Tom McGuire, Larry Steers, Elinor Vanderveer, Jack Grey, Bill Elliot, Florence Wix, Margaret Mann.

Released August 1, 1931
Running Time: 72 minutes.
Warner Brothers
Black and White

Broadminded is one of the weakest Joe E Brown films from this period, despite some elements that make it generally interesting from a historical perspective. First, it is oddly amusing to see Hungarian-born Bela Lugosi playing a Latin American character named Pancho, and trying to make a Spanish accent believable. And, it is one of the few appearances by actress and singer Marjorie White, who achieved continued notoriety due to her appearance with The Three Stooges in their first Columbia short a few years later, but whose career was cut short in a fatal car accident in 1935.

However, as a film, *Broadminded* offers little, even though it was penned by songwriters Bert Kalmar and Harry Ruby, who certainly had a flair for comedy. They also wrote the Marx Brothers' hilarious *Animal Crackers* (1930).

There might be some sociocultural interest in the way *Broadminded* presents the whims of the frivolous entitled types during

Bela Lugosi, Marjorie White, and Joe in Broadminded

Depression America, and the movie runs a compact and succinct 72 minutes, but it still comes off as weaker than any of the previous Joe E. Brown movies.

The film opens with a group of rich young upstarts holding a "baby party" in which everyone is clad in baby clothes. Joe, playing Ossie Simpson, enters in an oversized buggy and wearing a bonnet. He spends his entire first scene speaking in high pitched baby talk, slurping on a bottle, and making everyone around him laugh heartily even though he never says anything particularly funny. The cops break up the party, and Ossie's cousin Jack (William Collier) comes home staggeringly drunk. This upsets his father (Holmes Herbert) who orders that he get away from his New York life of gambling, drinking, and carousing for a while. He asks Ossie to be his chaperone, believing him to be a good example, not realizing he is every bit as much the drinker and carouser. They head to California, making several stops on the way. At one of the stops at a diner, they spill ink on the food of hot tempered Pancho, who becomes irate. This results in an amusing running gag where they keep running into Pancho throughout their journey.

When *Broadminded* opened in theaters, the movie's co-scripter Harry Ruby gave an interview to the press, stating:

> It is important to create sympathy for the comedian," says Harry Ruby of Kalmar and Ruby, the noted authoring team which wrote Joe E. Brown's latest starring vehicle, *Broadminded*. He continues: "Careless handling of the story will make him appear to be a fool, while in the best comedy he must simply be the unwitting victim of circumstances which he started in motion with the best of intentions, but which miscarry or backfire." That is exactly the comedy-making plan that Kalmar and Ruby used in devising *Broadminded*, and as a result Brown's new character has sympathy throughout the ludicrous troubles that he unintentionally brings on himself. This simple fellow, the sort one smiles at on sight, contrives a scheme to bring about a certain desirable end, a scheme he "prides himself on as being very clever, but an unforeseen factor comes in, upsets it and leaves him in an absurd mess. The result is little short of tragic to him, but very funny to onlookers.[11]

This is a very curious bit of publicity because in *Broadminded*, Joe is clearly a bumbler, not a sympathetic character.

There was an idea that Depression-era moviegoers, who were struggling with hard times, did not want to see more of the same in movies. Movies were inexpensive entertainment, so poor people could scrape up enough coins to attend the theater and forget about their situation. They also enjoyed seeing the problems of the rich and entitled, allowing them to escape their limited means into a world of privileged opulence. They wanted to escape the bleakness of the real world, which is why musicals and comedies were so popular. There is no music in *Broadminded* (even though the screenwriters, Kalmar and Ruby, were chiefly known as songwriters). But there also aren't many laughs.

---

11 Joe E. Brown's New Picture. *Democrat and Chronicle*. Rochester, NY. July 26, 1931

Joe and Thelma Todd in Broadminded

Perhaps the highlight is when Ossie is locked out of his room and has to run through the hotel in his underwear, believing Pancho is chasing him. In fact, Pancho is just trying to catch up to him and explain that all conflicts have been explained to him and there are no hard feelings. It is similar to the chase-on-foot sequence in the previous *Sit Tight*, which had also been that film's highlight.

Lugosi is indeed very funny here. It's interesting because in some ways his performance isn't all that different here than it is in *Dracula*, but he uses things like his serious glare for comedic effect, and it works well (even if it's hard to believe that he's supposed to be from Latin America). And, it is always worthwhile to see an early appearance by the delightful Thelma Todd, even though she is given little of interest to do in this script.

It is understood that while some older movies do not hold up as well after many decades have passed, comedy is usually timeless. But in the case of *Broadminded*, it isn't even a situation that seemed funny then but just doesn't work as well in the 21s century. Critics at the time were quite underwhelmed by this movie:

Things are very dull, very dull indeed, in the latest of Mr. Joe E. Brown's so-called comedies, something punningly labeled *Broadminded*. A couple of song-writers, Bert Kalmar and Harry Ruby, turned the thing out, obviously between, breakfast and golf, and it represents low humor at its unfunniest. Of course, Mr. Brown, as usual, strives mightily to help matters along with that wide grin and hog call of his, both of which he employs too often for comfort, but after possibly a half-dozen pictures of nothing more than wide grins and hog calls, one may be forgiven for growing a trifle bored with them all. The early promise of this erstwhile comedian, appears to have been sadly dissipated in a host of inferior productions, and his current release is one of the chief offenders.[12]

To be fair, along with Brown, everyone in the cast is doing their best with the lackluster material. Bela Lugosi, who would later indicate in interviews that he enjoyed doing comedies, even disdainfully mimics Joe E's wide-mouthed yell. But, as the above review claims, *Broadminded* is indeed quite dull.

What the critics could not realize is that *Broadminded* was the last Joe E. Brown film before he truly hit his stride and began refining his character for the screen and offering some consistently strong comedies. Joe himself was the reason. After finishing *Broadminded* Joe took the leading role in a Los Angeles stage production of *Elmer The Great*. This was a genuine role where he not only got to play comedy, but he also got to act. Brown decided he was tired of simply relying on his big mouth, his wild yells, and simple slapstick for his movies. He no longer wanted to bank off his vaudeville comedy and transition it to movies. The experience doing *Elmer The Great* on stage had caused him to become more interested in acting itself, so he now wanted to play characters with substance, adding dramatic element to narrative. And that began with his next effort, *Local Boy Makes Good*.

---

12 Broadminded Review. *Pittsburgh Post-Gazette*. July 6, 1931.

LOCAL BOY MAKES GOOD

Directed by Mervyn LeRoy
Screenplay: Robert Lord, Raymond Griffith, Ray Enright, and Walter DeLeon suggested by the play *The Poor Nut* **by J.C. Nugent and Elliott Nugent**
Cinematography: Sol Polito
Film Editing: Jack Killifer

Cast:
Joe E. Brown, Dorothy Lee, Ruth Hall, Edward Woods, Edward J. Nugent, Wade Boteler, John Harrington, William Burgess, Lee Phelps, Maude Eburne, Allan Lane, Edward Hearn, Curtis Benton.

Released November 27, 1931
Running Time: 68 minutes.
Warner Brothers
Black and White

Local Boy Makes Good is often referred to as the film that really begins Joe E. Brown's string of successful features that made him a top level star. This is true. But it is his role, and his approach to it, that make the film interesting. Joe E. Brown, as he'd requested, got to play a character that was more layered and more of a challenge in *Local Boy Makes Good*. However, there are times when the results are so heavily dramatic, it upsets the comedy potential. His character is so meek, and leans so heavily on pathos, he sometimes becomes more pathetic than sympathetic. But a dramatic element is what Joe wanted, and his more developed character did not go unnoticed by the press:

> *Local Boy Makes Good*; what a title of the next Joe E. Brown production! And what special news concerning it!

Joe of the giant grin will offer some genuine dramatic acting in the picture something, we learn, that he has wanted to do for quite a while. Lloyd Bacon has been named as director of the piece and camera action will be called within the next couple of weeks. Oh yes, let's give the writer a break. This one is an original by Walter Deleon of the First National staff.[13]

Shooting began in June. Lloyd Bacon, who had successfully directed Joe in the past, was first choice for director. Mervyn LeRoy was finally hired.

According to the newspapers, a schedule change necessitated a change of directors for the Joe E Brown film:

> Mervyn Le Roy has been assigned to direct *Local Boy Makes Good*, the new Joe E. Brown starring vehicle which is almost ready to start production at the First National studios in Burbank. This assignment was first given to Lloyd Bacon, the plan at that time being to produce *Local Boy Makes Good* after the completion of *The Honor of the Family*, the Bebe Daniels picture on which Bacon is now working. With the decision to put *Local Boy Makes Good* ahead on the schedule a change in director became necessary

Mervyn LeRoy began work on *Local Boy Makes Good* after finishing the heavy drama *Five Star Final* with Edward G. Robinson and Boris Karloff.

Casting the female roles was a bit of a challenge, with Evelyn Knapp cast, then replaced by Lillian Bond, and, finally Dorothy Lee. Dorothy has been working at RKO in the comedies of Bert Wheeler and Bob Woolsey, and had just finished work co-starring with Wheeler in his wrongheaded solo project *Too Many Cooks* (1931). The other female role in *Local Boy Makes Good* was taken by Ruth Hall. According to the press:

> Ruth Hall, the Florida girl who won recognition after eighteen months of extra work when Paramount executives cast her for the feminine lead in the Marx Brothers' *Monkey Business*, moves her makeup box over to the Vita-

---
13 Joe Brown's New One Demands Real Acting. *New York Daily News*. May 12, 1931.

phone studios this week to play an important role in Joe E. Brown's *Local Boy Makes Good*. Ruth, it now becomes known, piled up her dollars doing other duty while working as an extra. She played a part in the California production of *Once in a Lifetime,* which indirectly brought about her discovery.[14]

Trade ad for Local Boy Makes Good

Joe plays the very timid John Miller, a college botany student who works at a campus bookstore. John is infatuated with Julia Winters (Dorothy Lee), a coed whom he longs for from afar. He has been writing love letters to her, with no intention of ever sending one. However, when they are accidentally mailed, she reads them and concludes he is a campus track star. In order to save face, and on the advice of his pal Marjorie (Ruth Hall), John tries to join the

---
14 Irene Thirer column. *New York Daily News.* June 8, 1931

John Harrington and Joe in Local Boy Makes Good

track team. However, he turns out to be so inept with the javelin, he nearly injures star runner Wally Pierce (Edward J. Nugent), who chases him off the field. The track coach notices how fast John can run, and invites him to join the team in that capacity. He ends up running against Julia's old boyfriend, Spike (Edward Woods), and, through a series of circumstances, finally realizes that his pal Marjorie is really the girl for him.

The character Joe plays is a far cry from the brash, carousing type he had portrayed in other films, and while *Local Boy Makes Good* has its flaws, it is still a very important movie in the comedian's career. Playing the timid, insecure type, Brown tapped into another aspect of his screen persona that would be developed over time. In subsequent films, Brown would include elements of the brash upstart along with aspects of the timid bumbler, and come off as both funny, sympathetic and triumphant.

Of course the character does ultimately triumph in the movie but needs to learn about himself, and those around him, as he proceeds. The basis is not unlike Harold Lloyd's classic *The Freshman* (1925) in which the comedian is a put upon college student who proves himself in the big football game at the end. Joe E. Brown would revisit this concept some years later for his film *The Gladiator* (1938).

There are some isolated highlights in *Local Boy Makes Good* at least one of which takes advantage of the pre-code freedoms. Julia is a psychology student who appears to be quite interested and titillated by the sexual content of some of the lectures. She wants to give John more confidence and wrestles him around while discussing things like his "libido," while the shocked botany student reacts. It not only allows Joe E. Brown to further explore his character, but gives Dorothy Lee a fun set-piece to perform. By this time, Dorothy was quite well known by moviegoers as the Wheeler and Woolsey girl, and no stranger to bombastic comedy. In her later years she would look back on this project with fondness, stating:

> Joe E. Brown was wonderful. He was such a sweet, kind man. He would often go out of his way to help me do a scene, and it was a lot of fun working with him.[15]

The other highlights are the track scenes which offer the same sort of excitement and triumph as found in similar films like the afore-mentioned *The Freshman* as well as Buster Keaton's *College* (1927). Brown, like Keaton, was very athletic, so, also like Keaton, it was a bit of a hard sell to play a meek, unathletic man. When

---

15 Brotheron, Jamie and Ted Okuda. *Dorothy Lee: The Life and Times of the Wheeler and Woolsey Girl.* Jefferson, NC: McFarland. 2013

donning a track suit, both men are quite muscular and in top physical condition. The track scenes are great because they manage to be successful at being both thrilling and funny, such as when Brown falsely starts and runs the entire race before it has even officially started, then still manages to outrun everyone the second time

Local Boy Makes Good went on location in Lincoln, Nebraska to shoot some of the track scenes, amidst much local publicity. The city's newspaper stated:

> Those attending the A. A. U. track and field games July 3-4 may later see themselves in the movies. Joe E. Brown, film comedian, and a company if Hollywood actors, will be here to film the meet as a background for Brown's next picture, to be named *Local Boy Makes Good*. This information came from Carlisle Logan- Jones, a local boy who went to Hollywood and made good in the publicity department of Warner Brothers. A comedy race between Brown and Frank Wykoff will be staged Friday, July 3, as part of the picture. Director Mervyn LeRoy with the cast and crew of cameramen will leave Los Angeles Tuesday. Other shots of the various races and finishes will be made and used in later pictures which require a flavor of track and field.[16]

The newspaper also printed a follow-up story after the cast and crew arrived to proceed with their plans to film on the location:

> Nattily attired in a navy blue coat, light flannel trousers, sport shoes and a panama hat, Joe E. Brown, famous movie comedian, made his appearance Friday morning at Memorial stadium where scenes for his newest comedy, *Local Boy Makes Good* will be filmed during the national A. A U. track and field championships Friday and Saturday. Brown, Director Mervin LeRoy and Eddie Woods, "villain" of the picture, arrived in Lincoln at 2 a. m. Friday, following an appearance in an Omaha theater Thursday night.[17]

---

16 Joe E. Brown, Movie Comedian, To Use A. A. U, Games Here As Locale For His Next Screen Appearance. *Lincoln Journal Star*. June 26, 1931

17 Brown, Movie Clown Ready For Film Scene Here. *Lincoln Journal Star*. July 3, 1931

Dorothy Lee didn't make the trip, and was replaced by a double, Dorothy Dworak, a Nebraskan local who was chosen by location manager W.L. Guthrie. According to the press:

> Her work, as explained by Guthrie, will be to rush from the stands, throw her arms around Brown's neck and give him a big kiss as a reward for Brown's victory in a race. And what a race! "You really haven't seen a race until you see Joe in action," Guthrie said. Miss Dworak was not suffering from any illusions of grandeur after her selection. "I expect to have a lot of fun out of this, but that's all. I'm not figuring on rushing to Hollywood and push Marlene Dietrich, Greta Garbo and Bebe Daniels out of the limelight. I have too many interests in Nebraska.[18]

Local Boy Makes Good was another big box office hit for Joe E. Brown, taking in more than double its production costs. And, as already indicated, it was the film with which Brown hit his stride as a comedian who was also an actor, not just an extension of his vaudeville act. He now had several directions in which he could go with his screen persona, and more than one approach to his work as a movie comedian.

---

18 Dorothy Dworak, Petite Blonde, Will Double For Dorothy Lee In Joe E. Brown's Picture At A. A. U. *Lincoln Journal Star.* July 2, 1931

FIREMAN SAVE MY CHILD

Directed by Lloyd Bacon
Screenplay: Robert Lord, Ray Enright, and Arthur Caesar from their story.
Cinematography: Sol Polito
Film Editing: George Marks

Cast:
Joe E. Brown, Evalyn Knapp, Lilian Bond, Guy Kibbee, Richard Carle, George MacFarlane, Frank Shellenback, Virginia Sale, Dickie Moore, Curtis Benton, Fredrick Burton, Eddie Graham, George Meeker, Larry Steers, George Ernest, Cliff Saum, Louis Robinson, Henry Otho, Polly Walters, Harry Tenbrook, Wade Boteler, Ben Hendricks jr, Ginger Connolly.

Released February 20, 1932
Running time: 67 minutes
Warner Brothers
Black and White

If *Local Boy Makes Good* is an important transitional film in Joe E. Brown's movie career, *Fireman Save My Child* is significant as being the first in what is now known as Brown's baseball trilogy. Joe was a massive fan of baseball and wanted to incorporate that into his work. Offscreen, he assembled an amateur team on the Warner Brothers lot who would engage in pickup games for recreation. But he also wanted to find a way to use baseball in his movies. Screenwriters Robert Lord, Ray Enright, and Arthur Caesar created a story about a firefighter who invents a bomb that puts out fires. His prowess in baseball is a means to finance and promote the invention. Joe liked the idea, so they expanded their story into a screenplay.

Upon completing *Local Boy Makes Good*, and before shooting commenced on *Fireman Save My Child*, Joe went on a vaudeville tour of the Midwest, where his homespun humor had many fans. Louella Parsons wrote in her column:

> I have changed my mind about personal appearances. I used to think any star who stepped off the screen and tried to make a speech needed a guardian. In Chicago dozens of people have asked me about Joe E. Brown. Joe can move right into the Windy City any time he wishes. He was fairly popular before he appeared in Chicago, but now he is a top notch favorite. Joe E. is booked to say how-de-do in Cleveland this week and after that its Hollywood and home for him. Warner Brothers have prepared a story called *Fireman Save My Child*. It's a baseball yarn authored by the town wit, Arthur Caesar, also Robert Lord and Ray Enright. Lloyd Bacon is assigned to direct Joe and to see that his comedy smile is in good working order.[19]

Brown had a couple of weeks rest upon returning to Hollywood from his two week vaudeville gig in Cleveland before shooting began on *Fireman Save My Child* in early November.

Brown plays Joe Grant, and within that character he incorporates the swaggering type he played in his earlier films like *Maybe It's Love*, and the folksy small town sort he had played in *Local Boy Makes Good*. Joe is quite confident about his prowess on the baseball field, but it's just a sideline to him, much to the chagrin of team manager Pop Devlin (Guy Kibbee). Joe is so good, he gets offers to play in the major leagues, but ignores them. Furthermore, whenever he hears a fire alarm, he runs off the ball diamond in the middle of a game and helps to put out the fire. In one of the film's early scenes, Joe does just that, while the other players, used to this reaction, all sit or lie down on the diamond and wait for their star player's return. Brown plays his character's confidence in such an earnest manner, his strutting and bragging is amusing and endearing rather than off-putting.

---

19 Parsons, Louella. Fireman Save My Child is next Joe E. Brown Talkie. Universal Syndicate. October 7, 1931

Joe divides his time between firefighting and baseball in Fireman Save My Child

Joe's girlfriend is Sally Toby (Evalyn Knapp) who convinces him to take an offer from one of the big league teams so he can present his firebomb idea in the big city and get some needed attention and financing. Joe does, and his adjustment to city life is fraught with the sort of conflicts one could predict. The difference is, when Joe is approached by a woman trying to take advantage, it isn't so much his innocence that causes him to be duped, it is his ego. He comfortably believes that certainly a woman would be interested in a star ball player like himself. She gets him to drain his bank account back home with the idea that an executive friend of his needs the money to promote his invention. Sally innocently wires him the money. Joe is even duped into proposing, causing real conflict when Sally later comes to visit.

Fireman Save My Child has a wild climax in which Joe goes to a bank to get financing and sets the banker's office on fire. He discovers he also grabbed the wrong bag in a lobby mixup and doesn't have his bombs. The fire spreads wildly just as Joe recovers his bombs and effectively puts it out. He also finds out the banker is a fan of

A contest promoting Fireman Save My Child

his baseball prowess who agrees to hurriedly get him to a World Series game, just in time to win.

Fireman Save My Child sets the tone for subsequent Joe E. Brown comedies, showing him as a rural boy who goes from being a big fish in a small pond, to the opposite in the throes of the big city. In most of these films it is his innocence that is challenged. That's the case with this film too, but he is also comfortably secure in his abilities. When the other team members scoff at him, he is ready to fight. But it is from the perspective of the small town scrapper not someone who truly understands or realizes how out of place he is. This is an interesting balance, and Joe plays it well.

There is something a bit more childlike about Joe's innocence in this movie. Perhaps because it didn't feel like there was a lot of conflict; Joe is great at baseball, a great inventor, and great at fighting fires, and he never expresses any doubt in his ability to do those things, so we know that he will be fine no matter what happens. The story is an interesting take on the usual baseball movie, however. Most of the time the protagonist is striving to achieve their dream of playing major league baseball. Here, Joe has the St. Louis Cardinals practically begging him to join their team, but he is rather indifferent and would rather fight fires.

While he enjoyed the success he achieved with the comedy he played, Joe E. Brown didn't rest on his laurels. Despite his folksy charm, which sustained him offscreen as well, Joe was serious about his craft and wanted to explore different opportunities he might have with his roles. He realized that comedy was his forte and he had generated a solid following, but he also wasn't satisfied with settling on a standard screen persona that would sustain him through a series of formulaic productions. In each of his films, Joe investigates another aspect to his character.

Fireman Save My Child was another huge box office hit, tripling its production costs at the box office. John Scott's review in *The Los Angeles Times* recognized Joe E. Brown's expanding versatility:

> Little by little Joe E. Brown's pictures grow in plot and diminish in downright slapstick farce. *Fireman Save My Child* is the latest concoction to serve comedian Brown's talents. Brown is the small-town baseball pitcher and a fireman, to boot. In fact, his love for smoke-eating almost ruins his baseball career. After perfecting a fire extinguisher bomb, he accepts an offer to play with the St. Louis Cardinals to secure money enough to put over his invention. Whenever he hears a siren, off he goes, chasing the fire, and this leads him into all sorts of difficulties, especially during a crucial world series game. As "Smokey" Joe Grant, Brown plays the dumb, trusting chap who leaves a sweet and pretty girl at home while he seeks his fortune in the city, and then falls into the clutches of a beautiful clinging-vine who spends his money as fast as he makes it. Throughout the picture there are scattered plenty of typical Joe E. Brown mannerisms, especially the weird wail which is like nothing so much as a fire siren. His antics on the ball diamond will provoke mirth from those who know their baseball technique. For instance, he pitches with a double wind-up, even with men on the bases. *Fireman. Save My Child* is probably the comedian's best effort to date. The comedian works with a competent cast in the new picture. Evalyn Knapp is the home girl, and Lillian Bond portrays the "other" lady. Both display charm in

copious quantities. Guy Kibbee is the bombastic manager of the St. Louis ball team, while others include Richard Carle, George Meeker, Andy Devine and Frank Shellenback, famous pitcher of the Hollywood ball club. The story and adaptation are the work of Robert Lord, Ray Enright and Arthur Caesar. Lloyd Bacon may be credited with a good job of direction.[20]

The very next day in the same newspaper, it was reported that a preview audience "roared so that you must have heard them in New York."[21]

There was another event at around this time that connects to Joe's love of baseball. According to author Wes D. Gehring, Joe E. Brown's baseball team played Buster Keaton's team at Wrigley Field in Los Angeles (not to be mistaken for the one in Chicago):

> The two baseball-obsessed comedians had also arranged playing time for such other Hollywood students of the national game as Clark Gable, The Marx Brothers, Laurel and Hardy, Jimmy Durante, and Wheeler and Woolsey. After the stars started the game, players from the chicago Cubs and the New York Giants would complete the action. The two Major League teams were on the West Coast for spring training.[22]

Joe E. Brown was pleased with his success and with his being allowed some creative input as to his projects and the characters he would play. The success of this film helped place him among the top ten box office stars for 1932. His next film, *The Tenderfoot*, once again cast him as a small town boy attempting to survive in the big city.

---

20 Scott, John. Comic Proves Versatile: Joe E. Brown Portrays Combination Fireman and Ball Player in New Film. *The Los Angeles Times*. February 13, 1932
21 Joe E. Brown Comedy Due For Release. *The Los Angeles Times*. February 14, 1932
22 Gehring, Wes D. *Joe E. Brown: Film Comedian and Baseball Buffoon*. Jefferson, NC: McFarland, 2006

THE TENDERFOOT

Directed by Ray Enright
Screenplay: Earl Baldwin, Monty Banks, Arthur Caesar based on the story by George S. Kaufman and Richard Carle
Produced by Bryan Foy
Cinematography: Greg Toland
Film Editing: Owen Marks

Cast:
Joe E. Brown, Ginger Rogers, Lew Cody, Vivien Oakland, Robert Greig, Ralph Ince, Marion Byron, Spencer Charters, Douglas Gerrard, Richard Cramer, Al Hill, Charles Sullivan, Bob Perry, Nat Pandelton, Charlotte Merriam, Zita Moulton, Ted Lorch, Allan Lane, Edith Allen, Lee Kohlmar, Joe Barton, John Larkin, Eddie Kane, Herman Bing, Ben Hall, George Chandler, Jill Dennett, Harrison Greene, George Davis, Dorothy Vernon, Harry Seymour, Walter Percival.

Released May 23, 1932
Running time: 70 minutes
Warner Brothers
Black and White

Joe E. Brown liked to keep busy between projects and plans were made for him to do a tour after *Fireman Save My Child*, but after a stint on stage he was put into another movie. As early as February, 1932 announcements started hitting the press:

> They have had Joe E. Brown cavorting about in all kinds of roles, out there at Warner Brothers-First National, and now, of all things, he is to play a cowboy. Warners have bought Earl Baldwin's *The Tenderfoot* for him.[23]

---

23 Joe E. Brown, Cowboy. *The Los Angeles Times*. February 9, 1932

As exhibitors were looking forward to Joe doing a tour, which further benefited their box office, a story came out explaining he was only postponing these plans:

> Discarding plans for his proposed tour of personal appearance within a year, Joe E, Brown will begin work sooner than had been planned on his next film, *The Tenderfoot*. Arthur Caesar, Monty Banks and Earl Baldwin are now at work on the screen treatment for this story of a Texas cow puncher at large in a big town. Feb. 23 is now named as the date for the start of production. Ray Enright is to direct. The comic may make the proposed personal appearance tour upon completion of *The Tenderfoot*.[24]

It was about a week later when more stories regarding Brown's proposed tour showed up in newspapers:

> Following the enormous success of his personal appearance tour last summer, during which he visited important cities of the Middle West and East, Joe, E. Brown plans to make a similar tour at the end of March, according to latest word from Hollywood. If the present project materializes, he will set out from the cinema capital as soon as his next picture, *The Tenderfoot,* has been completed and will visit approximately half a dozen cities before returning to Hollywood to make another film. At the moment Brown is starring in a stage production, *Square Crooks*, in San Francisco

Between movies, stage productions, and personal appearance tours, the busy comedian was working hard and his stardom continued to grow.

While two original story writers are credited, their contributions were actually separate sources. The movie was partially based on the Richard Carle play *The Tenderfoot* as well as the George S Kaufman play *The Butter and Egg Man*. The Carle play, in which he also starred, opened in Chicago in July 1903 and moved to New York City in February, 1904. It closed in April, 1904 after 81 perfor-

---

24 Plan Early Production of Joe E. Brown Film. *The Brooklyn Daily Eagle*. February 15, 1932.

Ginger Rogers and Joe E. Brown in The Tenderfoot

mances. Kaufman's *The Butter and Egg Man* opened at the Longacre Theatre in New York on September 23, 1925 and closed in April, 1926 after 243 performances.

The story features proud Texan Calvin Jones (Joe E. Brown), who arrives in New York City with his $20,000 life savings in tow. A couple of Broadway producers (Lew Cody and Robert Greig) talk him into buying into their show. When the show flops in its initial run, Jones decides to buy out the other producers, deluding himself into believing it's a good show, when the others realize it's a bomb. Jones talks another naive man into investing with him, and decides to put on the show himself. His star actress (Vivien Oakland) quits, so he recruits secretary Ruth Weston (Ginger Rogers) to take her place. Although the play is supposed to be a drama, it is done so ineptly the audience laughs through the entire show and it is hailed as a great comedy hit. Calvin Jones and his investors end up making a profit on the show, and some gangsters try to horn in. When he refuses, they kidnap Ruth. Calvin uses his Texas wits to rescue her and subdues the criminals. He then marries Ruth, and returns to his native Texas, continuing to produce shows for the rural folk.

The Tenderfoot features Joe E. Brown in the title role, and while he once again has a down home swagger and a security that shows him truly comfortable in his own skin, this time he doesn't have quite the same naivete as in *Fireman Save My Child*. This is established almost immediately. Calvin Jones gets off the train in New York and hollers "Whoopee! Hello New York," boisterously announcing his arrival. As he swaggers proudly through the train depot, he is taken as a rube by a couple of operators. However when they approach him, address him as Colonel, and ask where he's going, they are rebuffed in a manner that tells us Calvin isn't easily duped. When a couple of ladies approach him immediately after, and read the information he has identifying his baggage, we get this exchange:

> First Woman: Well if it ain't Calvin Jones. I heard you were getting in town today.
>
> Calvin: Where'd ya hear that?
>
> Second woman: Over at the barber shop, and they just rave about you.
>
> First woman: The manicurist was telling us what a sweet, lovable guy you were.
>
> Calvin: Are you girls going to be around that barber shop this afternoon?
>
> Both women: Yes
>
> Calvin: Well will ya drop in and contradict that rumor?

A bum who claims he is starving and tries to beg a dime off Calvin doesn't fare much better when the Texan produces a sandwich out of his pocket.

However while this tells us that Calvin isn't likely to be taken, his lack of knowledge in the big city is still established when he enters a diner and sees several similarly dressed cowboys facing away from him at the counter. When he hollers "Whoopee!" toward them, they all turn around and exhibit effete, swishy mannerisms while wearing eye makeup, causing Calvin to remark, "they might be cowboys but they ain't from Texas!" He's also a bit loud and free with the fact that he is carrying around $20,000 in cash, and that is what attracts the theater producers.

Calvin's confidence never wavers, and Joe plays him with a true gusto that makes him both compelling and amusing rather than off-putting. There is an underlying earnestness that is discernible with this type of character as portrayed by Brown, and that's what sustains audience interest. His character is layered. While he is secure and confident, he never leaves his small town values and adapts to big city cynicism. Throughout the film, he dictates letters to his mother. When he invests in some "city clothes" he announces they came with two pairs of pants, stating, "that's why I'm late, it took me a long time to get 'em both on!"

His confidence carries over to his decision to buy out the other producers of the show, despite everyone else telling him that it is a terrible idea, and in his quickly finding the other man to invest with him. For somebody who talks openly about his money (usually a sign of naiveté), he exhibits quite a few business smarts.

One of the more amusing moments has Calvin despondent over not having wardrobe for the show, when Ruth finds old Shakespearian costumes in the theater basement. Calvin is fine with using them, despite the incongruity. This is what causes the leading lady to quit. Clad in Shakespearian garb, she complains "I look like a horse." "Not when you're standing up," Calvin innocently replies.

In all of Joe E. Brown's comedies there is a serious moment where he discovers the truth, is hurt and angry, and vows to do something about it. And often there is a pretty girl who initially flirts with him as a come-on for whatever scheme, and ends up falling for him as he realizes he's been duped. That is the formula here, and it works effectively with a lot of good comic situations. This effectively concludes with Calvin subduing the crooks who kidnap Ruth by gathering up couple of six shooters and heading to their hideout. It has already been established that he is a crack shot with a pistol.

In one of the movie's biggest highlights, Calvin pursues the fleeing gangsters on horseback, riding through the busy New York streets, lassoing the driver out of the car, and hog tying him, causing the auto to crash. The other crooks attempt to flee, but Calvin uses his shooting prowess by firing at street lights, phone poles, etc, and causing them to tip and fall on the gangsters. The slapstick effect is delightful. The last shot shows Calvin and Ruth pushing a baby carriage in Texas. A shot inside the carriage shows three Joe E Brown lookalike babies! *Film Daily* stated, "this ends the movie with a big laugh that will keep the audiences talking on their way out of the theater."[25] The review in the *New York Daily News* was even more enthusiastic, stating:

> *The Tenderfoot* is the funniest comedy Joe E. Brown has appeared in to date. Ray Enright, the director, has made a speedy comedy which opens with a good laugh and, except for a few sentimental touches in the love scenes, continues its risible course to a howling finish. Brown makes Calvin a likable fellow as he swaggers into New York. He gets off the nifties of the dialogue effectively in between his love scenes with Ginger Rogers. Miss Rogers, looking prettier than ever, plays the producer's secretary in a straight dramatic manner that adds interest to the plot. Lew Cody seems perfectly at ease in the role of the shoe-string producer who calls everybody sweetheart and who ropes Calvin into his shaky theatrical enterprise.[26]

Joe E. Brown enjoyed strong support in this movie. Ginger Rogers was, at the time, going with Mervyn LeRoy who was employed at Warner Brothers. This is one of the reasons why she ended up working at that studio after starting out at RKO Radio Pictures.

---

25 The Tenderfoot review. *Film Daily*. May 22, 1932
26 Tenderfoot review. *New York Daily News*. May 21, 1932

Rogers and Brown enjoyed working together and she ended up his leading lady in his next movie as well. Lew Cody's career dated back into the early silent era. He was just starting to get his career going in talkies around this time, and comes off well in *The Tenderfoot*. Sadly, he died two years later. Robert Greig, standing over six feet tall and weighing over 300 pounds, is an imposing comic presence. Brown said to the press, "We certainly got a bargain. That's a lot of actor for the money."[27] Vivien Oakland could play either haughty or supportive, working with many great comedians of the era, including Laurel and Hardy, Edgar Kennedy, and Andy Clyde. She registers most effectively as the temperamental leading lady. A Canadian newspaper stated:

> For once In many a long moon, there was no mad scramble for a juicy role that was open In Joe E. Brown's current First National picture, *The Tenderfoot*, and Vivian Oakland who ultimately got the part, may well be designated a brave woman. There are many actresses who do not mind playing wholly unsympathetic roles as long as they have a chance to display real histrionic ability; but it is another matter to ask an actress to play a "ham" actress in a genuine hammy manner. Vivian Oakland is now finding out that it is harder to act badly than it is to do the real thing. She plays the part of the star of a theatrical company, and her outstanding characteristics are supposed to be a self-imposed fiery temperament, ill-fitting high-hatism and an unconscious lack of acting ability which takes the form of over-acting.[28]

The Tenderfoot was another big hit, and at this point Warner Brothers realized they had discovered the best way to use their popular comedy star. The studio started to make arrangements to buy the film rights to *Elmer The Great*, which Joe appeared in successfully on stage. But in the meantime, Joe was placed in another vehicle to suit his talents, *You Said a Mouthful*.

---

27 Joe E Brown has Heavy Support in The Tenderfoot. *Marshall Evening Chronicle* June 29, 1932
28 Dominion Theater. *Victoria Daily Times*. June 26, 1932

YOU SAID A MOUTHFUL

Directed by Lloyd Bacon
Screenplay: Robert Lord and Bolton Mallory based on a story by William B. Dover
Produced by Raymond Griffith
Cinematography: Richard Towers
Film Editing: Owen Marks

Cast:
Joe E. Brown, Ginger Rogers, Preston Foster, Allen Clayton "Farina" Hoskins, Harry Gribbon, Edwin Maxwell, Sheila Terry, Oscar Apfel, William Burgess, Guinn "Big Boy" Williams, A.S. "Pop" Byron, Spencer Bell, Mia Marvin, Don Brodie, Eddy Chandler, Wilfred Lucas, June Gittelson, James Eagles, Bess Flowers, Anrhony Lord.

Released December 8, 1932
Running time: 70 minutes
Warner Brothers
Black and White

By the time he was ready to begin filming *You Said a Mouthful*, Joe E. Brown was basking in the massive stardom his films had afforded him. His love of sports became known to the point where he was asked to be Master of Ceremonies at a Rose Bowl event. While attending the subsequent game, his name was announced at the stadium and the fans all applauded and looked for him. He stood up and pointed to himself with his big smile, causing an even louder response from the crowd.

Unfortunately it was Joe's love of sports that resulted in his suffering a back injury that landed him in the hospital for weeks. Having earlier injured his back while doing his acrobatic act in vaudeville, Joe suffered a recurrence of that injury while playing baseball. This caused the filming of *You Said a Mouthful* to be delayed. When *You Said a Mouthful* was released, Joe E. Brown responded to the press regarding the injury:

> Joe E. Brown is back. Back in what is claimed to be his greatest comedy hit of all time, *You Said a Mouthful*. Back from a hospital siege where the sawbones chopped out his appendix, two or three vertebrae, and almost everything else except his funny bone. It was there to stay. And now Joe is here again with more pep, verve and elan than he has ever displayed before. "There's nothing funny about a hospital," said Joe, "but it makes you want to whoop and holler and raise Cain when you get out, you're so glad. The reaction makes you want to stir up a lot of fun."[29]

Joe E. Brown also returned to making personal appearances. The day after Christmas in 1932, Joe made a personal appearance at a home for delinquent boys. While other stars would donate money to such charities, Brown showed up in person and entertained these youngsters, giving them a happy Christmas.

You Said a Mouthful has Joe playing another meek, easily duped type with big ideas that are dismissed as silly by his employer. Coming off playing the swaggering character in *The Tenderfoot*, Joe's character in *You Said a Mouthful* was closer to the role he played in *Local Boy Makes Good*. Working for a rubber factory in the office, Brown plays Joe Holt, a mild mannered, whispery voiced fellow who has invented a floating swimsuit. However, his employer has no interest at all. His office workers are constantly playing pranks on the trusting Joe, and mock up a note supposedly from the boss indicating an interest in the invention. When Joe discovers it is all a ruse, much to the amusement of his co-workers, he is crestfallen as well as angry. Shortly thereafter, Joe is visited by a lawyer who indicates his aunt in California has died and left him her million dollar fortune. Joe quits his job and heads to the coast, but when he arrives, he discovers his aunt was actually broke, and all he inherits is a few dollars and the charge of, Sam, a young orphan boy (Farina).

---

29 Brown's First Since Illness Opens Sunday. *Kingsburg Recorder*. January 5, 1933

Ginger Rogers and Joe E. Brown dig into a watermelon in this promo shot for You Said a Mouthful

Meanwhile, there is another Joe Holt (Guinn Williams) who is a championship swimmer and is headed to that area to participate in an important swim to Catalina Island. Alice Brandon is sent to meet Joe Holt but when she pages him, she is met by meek Joe the hapless inventor. Before he realizes what's going on, Joe is committed to the swim meet, but believes his floating swimsuit will sustain him. Sam, who is a very good swimmer, helps him as well. Of course there are complications, the swimsuits get mixed up, and in spite it all, Joe wins the meet and Alice's hand.

Ginger Rogers, who enjoyed working with Joe in *The Tenderfoot*, was pleased to be reunited with him for this film, but would soon make an even greater impact in *42nd Street* (1933). And the producer of the film, Raymond Griffith, had once been a highly skilled movie comedian in silent films, but his career did not survive talkies, despite his noted performance in the Oscar winner *All Quiet on the Western Front* (1930). But it is the appearance of Allen Clayton Hoskins, aka Farina, that stands out. Farina had been one of the most popular kids in producer Hal Roach's Our Gang comedies,

Allen Clayton Hoskins, Farina in Our Gang, was branching out into features when he appeared with Joe in You Said a Mouthfull

but had grown out of his role. He cut off the braids in his hair, and sought work in feature films. Warner Brothers was, at the time, one of the studios more accepting to hiring African American actors, and Farina secured a contract there. He and Joe E. Brown work well together to the point where Farina can be considered a full co-star.

Along with being very funny providing the film with even more comic relief, Farina does not play the sort of stereotypical comic role in which we see most African American supporting actors at this time in Hollywood. His character isn't portrayed as stupid or scared. The humor comes straight from him, not from the white characters making fun of him.

The cast of *You Said a Mouthful* was rounded out by Preston Foster as Ed Dover, a wise guy rival in the swim meet, and Harry Gribbon as Harry Daniels, Joe's nemesis at the office who ends up working with Dover at the swim meet. Gribbon was already a long time comedy movie veteran, having worked in Mack Sennett comedies during the teens with the likes of Fatty Arbuckle and The Keystone Cops. While Gribbon made a successful transition to sound films, he stopped acting in movies by the end of the 1930s, even though he lived until 1961. Preston Foster was a Broadway actor who would be better known for more serious dramatic roles. But he would also appear in Joe E. Brown's next movie, *Elmer The Great*.

Unfortunately, *You Said a Mouthful*, while amusing, is not at quite the level of Joe's previous movies. It has all of the elements that sustained other Brown comedies, including Joe beating the odds and emerging victorious in the end. But it seems to move a bit more slowly, and drag in some parts, where his better films were tighter. A review in *The New York Daily News* noticed the difference, while also acknowledging Farina's contribution:

> The film runs a bit too long, over-emphasizing certain sequences toward the end. But it is nicely built on gags. And the acting by the inimitable Joe E. and his supporting cast is swell in the laugh line. There's the return appearance of none other than Allen Hoskins who won hearts the world over as the Farina of Our Gang. Farina is quite a big boy now, and he's a dandy trouper. In fact, his part is second in importance to the star's.

Farina would appear in only two more Warner Brothers features -- *The Life of Jimmy Dolan* with Douglas Fairbanks jr, and *The Mayor of Hell* with James Cagney (both 1933) before his contract ran out. He made only a few fleeting appearances after that as a freelancer. Farina enlisted in the army during World War Two, saw action in five Pacific battles, rose to the level of Sergeant, and received a Presidential citation. When he returned home, he expected to return to movies as an actor but couldn't find work. He later went into the medical field, working with people who had cognitive disabilities.

Much of the swimming scenes were filmed on location at Catalina Island, but actual sharks became a problem at one point. According to this article:

> A shark sent Joe E. Brown and a score of swimmers scurrying for the shore during the taking of a scene for his latest First National comedy, *You Said a Mouthful*, which is on the screen of the New Santa Cruz theater today. The main action of the picture revolves around a marathon

swimming race in which Joe is induced to enter through a series of comical errors, although he had never before swum a stroke. These scenes were taken off Catalina Island, where sharks occasionally put in an appearance. Joe is supposedly attacked by a shark in the picture, but when the players saw a fin cut the water some hundred yards from shore,, they knew it was no film prop fish. There was a yell of "shark" and everyone struck out for shore.[30]

You Said a Mouthful was another big box office hit for Joe E. Brown, and maintained his top level stardom. Warner Brothers had, by now, secured the movie rights to Joe's stage success *Elmer The Great* and arrangements were made for that to be Joe's next movie.

---

30 Shark Cuts Short Filming of Joe E. Brown Scene. *Santa Cruz Evening News*. December 26, 1932

ELMER THE GREAT

Directed by Mervyn LeRoy
Screenplay: Thomas Geraghty based on a play by Ring Lardner and George M. Cohan
Produced by Raymond Griffith
Cinematography: Arthur L. Todd
Film Editing: Thomas Pratt

Cast:
Joe E. Brown, Patricia Ellis, Frank McHugh, Claire Dodd, Preston Foster, Russell Hopton, Sterling Holloway, Emma Dunn, Charles C. Wilson, Charles Delaney, Berton Churchill, J. Carroll Naish, Gene Morgan, Walter Miller, Douglass Dumbrille, Jessie Ralph, George Chandler, Gale Gordon, Jane Wyman, Maurice Black, Frank O'Connor, Paul Kruger, Don Brodie, Harrison Greene, Charles Sherlock, Gary Usher, Lloyd Neal, Gary Usher, John Sheehan, Leo White, Fred Santley

Released April 29, 1933
Running time: 72 minutes
Warner Brothers
Black and White

Elmer the Great is not only the best Joe E. Brown movie thus far, it is one of his best movies overall. Part of the reason is that Brown played the title role in the stage version and thus was familiar with the character, which he had already developed over several performances. the play opened on Broadway in September of 1928 with Walter Huston in the title role. It ran 40 performances before closing on Broadway and going on the road. Joe had played the role in a couple of different Los Angeles-based companies in 1930 between acting jobs in movies.

Ad for Elmer The Great

Joe E. Brown had honed the character with elements of actual baseball players he had known. This included Dizzy Dean of the St. Louis Cardinals, who was boastful but whose prowess on the diamond lived up to the hype. Joe also utilized the swagger of past ball player Frank Coveleski. According to Wes D. Gehring:

During Brown's vaudeville days, he closely followed Coveleski's career and was fascinated by the player's goofy lumbering walk, a sort of lazy swagger with prominent arm swinging. The comedian adopted the gait and deliberate mannerisms for his take on Elmer.[31]

Because of this background, Joe E. Brown was more comfortable in this role than any other. Of course its stage trappings were expanded for the screen, and there were some changes, the most significant being the change of Elmer's talent from pitching to batting.

The story deals with Elmer Kane (Joe E. Brown), a small town boy whose talents are so vast, he is recruited by the Chicago Cubs. His skills are matched by his ego, but despite his boastful manner, Elmer is also naive and an apt patsy for practical jokes. The team management scolds the team, indicating that Elmer is winning the games for them, and they are to make him feel comfortable. He is terribly connected to his home town, so baseball managers never give him letters his girl Nellie (Patricia Ellis) sends him, fearing he will quit and return home. Elmer is briefly taken advantage of by an actress (Claire Dodd) and visiting Nellie finds them in a compromising position that she doesn't realize is innocent. Hurt, she storms off and the situation angers Elmer who ends up in a gambling house incurring a huge debt. The casino owner indicates he will erase the debt if Elmer purposely plays badly in the World Series, resulting in a heavy gambling win. A fight ensues, Elmer ends up in jail, but makes up with Nellie and is released in time to join the big game, which is being played through a rainstorm. However, he isn't allowed in the game because it is discovered that he accepted the gangsters' bribe. When it is discovered that he bet on his own team to win, the management realizes Elmer is actually planning to double cross the gangsters, is allowed in the game, and wins.

In no previous film did Joe E. Brown command the screen more forcefully than in *Elmer The Great*, and this is evident in the opening scenes. Elmer sleeps until 2pm, then gets up and has an enormous breakfast with eggs, pancakes, ham, donuts, and fruit, washed down with a tall glass of milk. He struts about, firmly connected to his surroundings, happy to be living in his mother's house, in a small town, with an ordinary job in a store. That's all he wants. And while he has a pretty sizeable ego about his baseball prowess,

---

31 Gehring, Wes D. *Joe E. Brown: Film Comedian and Baseball Buffoon.* Jefferson, NC: McFarland, 2006

he has no interest in venturing beyond his immediate surroundings. He is comfortable. He has no dreams. When the Cubs representative comes to get him, he gets rebuffed by Elmer. It takes Nellie to goad him into taking the opportunity.

Elmer is similar to Joe's character in *Fireman Save My Child* in this way: becoming a major league baseball player, a dream for so many, isn't a priority for him, and his skill at the game comes easily to him. Sterling Holloway is enjoyable, especially the scene where he tries to convince Elmer to join the team, and is in disbelief when Elmer refuses. It provides good context for how strange that sort of behavior seems to most people. But even outside of being great at baseball, in those opening scenes we see everything else in his life coming easy to him, such as his mom waiting on him hand and foot. The opening shots effectively set up what a small town Elmer lives in, when the Cubs manager tells the operator that he is coming to see Elmer but not to tell anyone, but of course she does and the word spreads very quickly.

The scenes once he begins working out with the ball club show Elmer's naivete as much as his ego. He wonders why someone with his skill needs to work out among the rookies. He can't understand why he, himself, is considered a rookie. What is remarkable is that his braggadocio is not hollow; it is backed up by performance. Elmer smacks every ball he is pitched, causing it to sail over the fence.

Of course the original play is expanded for movies by having the distraction of crooks trying to take advantage of the skillful rube, and Elmer's betting on his own team, although double-crossing the crooks, would be quite illegal in real life. But this is where fun is more important than logic. Elmer's winning of the big game is given the dramatic element of pouring rain and splattering mud, adding a bit of razzle-dazzle to the visual imagery and some extra excitement to the climactic scenes. Director Mervyn LeRoy does a nice job of seamlessly intercutting actual baseball footage with the staged scenes for the Brown comedy.

There are a few interesting ideas inserted into the final game. Because of the rain, the opposing team's pitcher and catcher work out a routine where the pitcher moves his arm but doesn't really throw a ball, and the catcher punches his mitt as if he's caught one.

This results in two strikes on Elmer. Savvy to their ruse, Elmer then steps in front of the plate to prove no ball has been thrown.

We are reminded that *Elmer The Great* is a pre-code movie where restrictions were not too heavily enforced, when Elmer is told to warm up and he responds, "Warm up? Hell, I haven't been cold since February!" There was the occasional "hell" and "damn" in the dialog of movies before the Production Code was more heavily restrictive after 1934.

Sympathy is drawn to Elmer's character via a tangential scene where he is duped into appearing on the radio. He takes it seriously, sending out a heartfelt message to his mother. When he discovers it was all a gag, his feelings are hurt. Elmer has no real understanding of practical jokes, and little sense of humor about himself. When he is briefly jailed for the mixup with gamblers, he refuses release when bailed out. He just stays in his cell and sleeps, a way of distancing himself from his many immediate problems.

Elmer The Great was an enormous success at every level. Critics referred to the film as "comic perfection," while theatrical exhibitors in the trades reported that their audience laughed and cheered throughout the screenings. A report from Radio City Music Hall indicated that the packed house sat in rapt attention during the climactic baseball scene. And, despite the afore-mentioned cuss word in the dialog, the exhibitors praised the movie as clean entertainment for the patrons. For the remainder of his life, Joe E. Brown would cite *Elmer The Great* as his favorite among his films.

Elmer The Great ignited a particularly strong series of Joe E. Brown films. He extended beyond the proven formula for a few films, and tried to expand his character. Joe E. Brown would continue to draw from the two opposing personalities he had presented on screen -- the swaggering braggart and the reserved milquetoast. His next, *Son of a Sailor*, presents his character as boisterous but, unlike Elmer, unable to back it up with action. It added a deeper layer to an established screen persona, and Brown's exploring it resulted in another one of his best films.

SON OF A SAILOR

Directed by Lloyd Bacon
Screenplay: Al Cohn and Paul Gerard Smith
Cinematography: Ira Morgan
Film Editing: James Gibbon

Cast:
Joe E. Brown, Jean Muir, Frank McHugh, Thelma Todd, Johnny Mack Brown, Sheila Terry, George Blackwood, Merna Kennedy, Kenneth Thomason, Samuel S. Hinds, Noel Francis, Arthur Vinton, George Irving, Ward Bond, Walter Miller, Purnell Pratt, Joe Sawyer, bobby Dunn, Lee Moran, George Chandler, Eddie Kane, Henry O'Neill, Edward Hearn, John Kelly, Garry Owen, John Marston, Jack Pennick, John "Skins" Miller.

Released December 23, 1933
Running time: 73 minutes
Warner Brothers
Black and White
Working title: *Son of the Gobs*

In a film like *Elmer The Great*, Joe E. Brown plays the title role as a swaggering braggart who can back up his conceit with successful action. In *Son of a Sailor* he is Handsome Callahan, a navy man aboard ship[32] who brags as boisterously, but without sufficient backup. Handsome is just a blowhard. In the film's opening scenes a boxing match has been set aboard ship and Handsome brags to his gullible friend Gaga (Frank McHugh) that he could handily beat either fighter: "You ever see the lump on Jack Dempsey's jaw? Next time you see Jack, ask him who put it there." Of course it is

---

32 Much of Son of a Sailor was shot on board the USS Saratoga with 100 navy men as extras.

highly unlikely Gaga will ever meet Jack Dempsey, so the boast will never be disproven. This is how Handsome operates.

When one of the fighters injures himself during work detail, Handsome is forced to take his place against a larger, more aggressive opponent. So he goes to the fighter's dressing room and offers him $50 to lay down in the second round. Handsome doesn't realize he went into the room of a preliminary fighter (who takes the money and does as instructed, but in a completely different match). Thus, Handsome must face his snarling opponent on his own merit.

This adds another layer to Joe E. Brown's braggart character. Unable to back up his claims as he could in *Elmer The Great* or *Fireman Save My Child*, Joe's character has to hastily come up with something within the situation in order to save face. What is interesting, though, is that the film doesn't simply rely on the predictable pattern of the empty promises being revealed and the character running scared throughout the fight. There is some of that during the boxing scene, but there are also many instances of Handsome gamely fighting back and landing several punches, including several upper cuts after a swinging wind-up. The problem here is that Handsome's opponent is so tough, he is unfazed by the aggressive attempts at fighting back.

The scene does conclude with Handsome winning on a fluke, his opponent being distracted by a bugle call and Handsome landing a wild punch, knocking the man out. So he saves face in order to maintain the character further into the narrative.

This is only an opening sequence to establish the Handsome character. He then leaves this setting, and goes ashore eventually getting mixed up with high ranking officials about whom he's bragged, and a spy ring that he capably thwarts. Thus, the trajectory of the character is that he is indeed capable of heroics when not distracted by his own boastfulness.

On shore, Handsome flirts with a series of different women, carrying a pair of baby shoes that he borrowed from a fellow Sailor named Duke who got them from his girlfriend Helen. One of the women he flirts with is Helen, who sees the inscription on the soles of the baby shoes and realizes Handsome's ploy. He continues to brag about his friendship with various admirals, not realizing that

Helen is also the daughter of his ship's admiral. He ends up at her home, where the top Navy brass are staying, and Helen tips them off about Handsome's bragging. To have a bit of fun, when they meet Handsome they all respond as if his wild tales about their past friendship were true ("remember when we did this...?"). The sequence where he tries to pick up different women is perhaps overlong, but it's effective in that we get to see how he changes his story around with each woman he meets. It's very amusing.

It is soon discovered that there are spies also in the home, ready to steal secret military plans. They do so, but it is Handsome who captures them. The head spy tries to get away by plane, but it is a remote control vehicle wired to return to the ship unless the controls are tampered with. Handsome prevents the pilot from doing so, and the plane does return to the ship and the spy is arrested. Handsome is decorated and given a promotion, promising to never lie again. The final scene shows him on shore leave in China, pulling the same ruse about the baby shoes on another innocent woman -- but this time speaking in Chinese!

There are many comic highlights in *Son of a Sailor* before its gratifying conclusion. First, Handsome tries to instruct Gaga on how to successfully romance a woman. Gaga sits on Handsome's lap, rests his head on his shoulder, and listens to his tender, loving words. Meanwhile, their shipmates quietly come out on deck and watch them until Handsome notices they're there and throws Gaga off. The others get a good laugh, and then hand Handsome a small box "from the Admiral." It contains a pansy!

The afore mentioned boxing match is another highlight, with good rhythmic editing to enhance both the action and the comic structure. Cutaways to Gaga getting so wrapped up in the action conclude with him hitting himself in the chin and knocking himself out. Meanwhile, during the bout, the camera shifts from low medium shots, to higher overhead ones, keeping all of the action within the frame. Director Lloyd Bacon's experience dated back to silent comedy, where he was an actor in some early Charlie Chaplin shorts during the comedian's transitional Essanay period. And, having helmed several Joe E. Brown features already, he knew how to effectively utilize his star's talents.

Joe and Frank McHugh made a fun team in Son of a Sailor

Handsome is accosted by a female member of the spy ring, played by Thelma Todd, who would take jobs in feature films while on break from her short subject series at the Hal Roach studios. Thelma had appeared in Joe's earlier film *Broadminded* but given comparatively little to do. She makes a fun comic impact in *Son of a Sailor*. Vamping it up as only she can, Thelma's feminine wiles and Handsome's fluttery, intimidated reaction is quite amusing. It also further reveals Handsome's lack of confidence in such situations despite his braggadocio.

And there is the wild climactic scene where Handsome goes after the spy who tries to escape by airplane with the stolen plans. As he runs toward the plane, Handsome trips, falls, and then stops to tie his shoe. By the time he reaches the plane, he has to grasp its tail, which causes him to go sailing into the sky. He climbs up onto the plane and hits the pilot with a large wrench, while getting his feet tangled in gear shift wires. This causes the plane to flip and fly before finally making it to shipboard. But only the spy is on board. Handsome has bailed out and landed on an abandoned ship that is being used as a target for bombing maneuvers. It's all very exciting, very funny, and nicely done.

The fact that Joe E. Brown was making his comedies for a big studio like Warner Brothers (through their First National production unit) allowed for these big sweeping gags to look especially effective. Better production costs were available to films made at the major studios, of course, while Joe's movies were such a box office success, the studio realized that spending a bit more to get a desired visual effect would pay off.

Critics applauded this Joe E. Brown vehicle as his funniest thus far, and moviegoers responded the same. John Scott stated in his review for *The Los Angeles Times*:

> All the ingredients of a typical Joe E. Brown screen comedy are found in *Son of a Sailor*. The piercing screech, swaggering walk and the funny face are very much present, but set in a new locale. As in other Brown productions, Joe E. dominates the plot and action, with supporting players providing the necessary atmosphere.
>
> As usual, this film moves along swiftly, true to the Brown comedy formula.[33]

Meanwhile, exhibitors in the trade magazine *Motion Picture Herald* reported good attendance and a great reaction from their audiences:

> Joe E. Brown's best. Did fair business through the nastiest weather we've had in many years.
>
> This is Brown's best comedy to date and played to packed houses both days.
>
> Here is a side splitting comedy with Joe E. Brown. Plenty of comedy, action, and a touch of romance. He is sure to keep the audience laughing from start to finish. One of the best comedies of the year.[34]

One exhibitor reported that a patron of his had previously told him the next time the theater showed a movie with "that big mouthed fella" he would bring a truckload of friends to see it. The

---

33 Scott, John. Joe E. Brown Turns Gob. *Los Angeles Times*. December 29, 1933
34 What The Picture Did For Me. *Motion Picture Herald*. March 24, 1934

Thelma Todd and Joe in Son of a Sailor

man kept his word when *Son of a Sailor* played that theater, and was given a free pass by the owner. *Son of a Sailor* was yet another box office success for Joe E. Brown, whose stardom continued with each new release.

Perhaps the only trifling quibble regarding *Son of a Sailor* is that it starts to develop an amusing relationship between Handsome and Gaga, but that is dropped shortly after the sailors go on shore. Frank McHugh had appeared in several of Joe's films and worked well with him. Frank would again play a brash sailor's pal in another Warner release, *Here Comes The Navy* (1934) starring James Cagney.

Buoyed by this film's success, but till wanting to branch out and investigate other possibilities in movies, Joe E. Brown's next film had him playing a character based on a Damon Runyon story. The result was, *A Very Honorable Guy,* an uncharacteristically dark comedy that did not please Brown's many fans, disrupting the momentum in his screen popularity.

A VERY HONORABLE GUY

Directed by Lloyd Bacon
Screenplay: Earl Baldwin from a story by Damon Runyon
Produced by Hal Wallis
Cinematography: Ira Morgan
Film Editing: William Holmes

Cast:
Joe E. Brown, Alice White, Robert Barratt, Alan Dinehart, Irene Franklin, Hobart Cavanaugh, Arthur Vinton, G. Pat Collins, Harold Hubert, James Donlan, Harry Warren, Al Dubin, Brooks Benedict, Matt Briggs, Maidel Turner, Billy West, Aggie Herring, Clarence Muse, Eddie Kane, Raymond Brown, Bud Jamison, Ernie Adams, Stanley Blystone, Wade Boteler, Sidney Bracey, James Burke, Jack Cheatham, Philo McCullough, Bob Montgomery, Richard Powel, Harry Semels, Robert Ellis, Al Hill, Charles Williams, Harry Holman, Katherine Ward, Paul Hurst, Larry Steers, Charles Sullivan.

Released May 4, 1934
Running time: 62 minutes
Warner Brothers
Black and White

A Very Honorable Guy is just the type of role Joe E. Brown wanted, but, unfortunately, his audience wasn't quite ready to allow him to stretch as an actor. This Damon Runyon story is essentially a serious one with Joe playing a character who doesn't fit any of the screen personae Brown had established. He wasn't a timid milquetoast nor was he an overconfident braggart. Joe was playing a specific character out of a Runyon story, and doing so rather straight. And while his performance is quite good, and the movie is overall well done, it is not the sort of film that had established Joe E. Brown's stardom.

Joe plays Feet Daniels, an unsuccessful Broadway gambler that is befriended by gangsters who use him as a patsy. In the latest instance, the gangsters want to rough up someone who owes their boss money, but he has barricaded himself in his apartment. Feet is instructed to knock on the door, realizing that he will be allowed in. Feet does so and the gangsters burst in and beat the man. Feet tries to intervene but is punched and falls into a closet. When he awakens and bursts out into the room, the gangsters have fled and Feet inadvertently punches one of the detectives who have arrived on the scene.

This early sequence establishes the character Joe E. Brown is playing as a straight part with few-to-none of the elements that define him on screen up to now. He is forthright and scrupulous, but unsuccessful and connected to a criminal element. And when he is arrested, it is the head gangster, The Brain, who bails him out. But that means Feet has to come up with the $500 bail money to

Joe and Alice White in A Very Honorable Guy

pay him back, or suffer the same fate as the man whom he saw get roughed up by The Brain's henchmen.

The narrative shifts when Feet decides to sell his body to science for $1000. He gets a wacky doctor (Robert Barratt) to give him the money and a couple of cyanide capsules to take on a certain day. This doctor has designs on Feet's girl Hortense (Alice White), so he'll be glad to have Feet out of the way. However, not long after this deal is made, Feet's luck changes and he starts to be consistently successful at gambling. Feet chooses winning sweepstakes tickets, makes bets that net wins, and before long he has generated enough money to pay all of his debts. Feet now wants out of the deal with the doctor, and offers to not only return his $1000, but will include another $1000 on top of it.

Joe E. Brown is much more subdued in this role, as is befitting the character. He never lets out his famous comic yell, and doesn't settle into his vaudeville schtick. If he is funny, it is his character responding to the situation. And it is the situation itself that is amusing.

There are several highlights. In one, Feet tries a drug store punch-pin game for five cents a shot in order to win a 10 dollar box of candy. He spends 10 dollars attempting to get a winner but with no luck. Shortly afterward, a woman comes into the store and, on impulse, tries the game and wins the candy immediately. Joe reacts of course, but subtly and within the framework of the scene. It is the situation that is amusing, and Joe's reaction is within the context of that situation.

And the realization that Feet has transformed from loser to winner occurs in an amusingly unwitting manner. Believing he is ordering sandwiches from a waiter, Feet calls out to the man running the dice game at a casino, "I'll take two." The man accepts "two thousand dollars on the next roll of dice." Feet tries to stop him, but the dice rolls, and the man makes the point. This happens again before Feet takes what has now built up to $16,000 and leaves the table. This is followed by a montage of Feet winning at several different games, finally enjoying a lofty position. The fact that he'd already cultivated a reputation of always paying his debts now pays off with the karma of him no longer needing money.

Of course Feet's euphoria is shot down when he suddenly realizes that he is days away from having to fulfill his agreement with the doctor, who won't let him back out. The fact that circumstances reveal the doctor to be crazy and the agreement void is indicated with a series of different situations. Actor Robert Barratt plays the doctor as slightly off-kilter throughout the film, including squirting copious amounts of ketchup into his coffee. Also, the climax involves Feet marrying Hortense on the day he was supposed to die, but it ultimately ends with them happily settling down on a chicken farm. Feet's dynamic with Hortense is interesting in that she was a lot more commanding and motivated by money than most of the characters who had served as the Joe E. Brown love interest up to now.

A Very Honorable Guy is a very pleasant, amusing movie and Joe E. Brown plays his role effectively. But because it was not his usual bombastic comedy, his fans were disappointed. Notes from exhibitors in *Motion Picture Herald* reveal how audiences reacted:

> The poorest Joe E. Brown picture to date.
> After the first show, a poor crowd, and that's that.
> Shame on you Joe. You never got a smile in this one.
> Brown is a favorite here and up until now he never missed but this is just a waste of time.
> They came for the first matinee and after that they went out and told everybody to stay away.[35]

While critics respected the film as something different, and it didn't do badly at the box office, *A Very Honorable Guy* was too offbeat to please most moviegoers. Still, *Film Daily* was quite positive about the film, stating: "While the plot idea in back of this picture is a bit stretched, it has enough laughs, action and suspense to provide fairly good satisfaction for the regular Joe E. Brown fans."[36]

It is unfortunate that audience reaction was enough to disrupt the box office success of *A Very Honorable Guy*. It showed Brown's ability to move away from his presence as a comedian, and develop an equally sound presence as an actor who could play comedy. Brown's

---

35 What The Picture Did For Me. *Motion Picture Herald*. April, 1934
36 Very Honorable Guy review. *Film Daily*. May 18, 1934

Robert Barrat and Joe in A Very Honorable Guy

secure, measured performance reveals levels of ability that extend beyond the skills he has provided in his comedies. Not that *A Very Honorable Guy* is a drama, but this comedy is a different approach, along with being a good movie with a fine performance by its star. The creative fulfillment that Joe E. Brown gained from his work on *A Very Honorable Guy* was sadly thwarted when audience reaction indicated that he needed to return to a more established formula.

Joe E. Brown was moved quickly into his next project, which had the working title of *Sawdust*. Joe was attracted to this circus story penned by Bert Kalmar and Harry Ruby, having had his own experiences, and liked the idea of playing the dual role a circus clown and well as his own father, a cynical veteran clown. He also liked that it was another comedy with a more subtle approach to the character and the situations. Because it was filmed immediately after production ended on *A Very Honorable Guy*, the studio was unaware as to the negative reaction that movie would generate. So Joe's next film, which was released as *Circus Clown*, again allowed him to branch out and explore what he could do as an actor.

CIRCUS CLOWN

Directed by Ray Enright
Screenplay: Bert Kalmar and Harry Ruby from their story
Cinematography: Sidney Hickox
Film Editing: Clarence Kolster

Cast:
Joe E. Brown, Patricia Ellis, Dorothy Burgess, Don Dillaway, Gordon Westcott, Charles C. Wilson, Harry Woods, Ronnie Cosby, John Sheehan, Spencer Charters, Tom Dugan, Earle Hodgins, Gordon Evans, Ward Bond, Poodles Hanneford, Lee Moran, Bertha Matlock, Alfredo Codona, Bernie Griggs, Jack Wise, Pat Kling, Jack McAfee, Ruby Woods, Mickie McDonald, Curley Phillips, Bill Kling, Bertha Matlock, Lorin Raker, Charles Redrick, Eddie Shubert, Renee Whitney, Milt Taylor, Tom Wilson.

Released June 30, 1934
Running time: 64 minutes
Warner Brothers
Black and White
working title: *Sawdust*

Joe E. Brown was about to take a tour of the Orient, along with his wife, and planned to leave in March. Thus, he was rushed very quickly into *Sawdust* after completing *A Very Honorable Guy* so that Warner Brothers would have product for theaters while Joe was out of the country for a few months. Titled *Circus Clown* upon its release, this latest Joe E. Brown feature was released less than two months after *A Very Honorable Guy* and shortly before Joe returned to America. In fact, its premiere screening was held in early June on the ship of the President Coolidge where passengers were able to enjoy the film before it played theaters later that month. Joe was on board this ship headed back to America.

It is no surprise why Joe was attracted to this screenplay. It allowed him to recall his acrobatic past, doing stunts in the movie he had

Joe as Happy the Clown in The Circus Clown

performed in circuses as a young man. This was not Joe's first circus movie, he had already done a silent, *The Circus Kid*. But this was his first opportunity to play in such a film after having achieved top level stardom. Joe was further attracted to the script because it allowed him to play two roles -- the journeyman clown Happy, and

Happy's father, who is a retired clown. The roles are both layered characters who are different from one another, but each has traits of Joe's established screen persona. This is the sort of acting challenge Joe craved, and yet was remarkably able to establish the nature of the relationship between them. They are both great performances.

The film was nicely mounted, offering an effective visual circus atmosphere. For authenticity, Warner Brothers hired actual circus performers to fill out some roles:

> Real circus personalities are to join *Sawdust"* in which Joe E. Brown will be starred as a circus clown with Patricia Ellis playing opposite. Poodles Hanaford, one of the most famous clowns, will take an important role while Alfredo Cordona of the famous Cordonas, will also be in the picture.[37]

It's worth noting that Hanaford, who was sometimes billed as "the Charlie Chaplin of the circus," appeared in some of his own silent comedies during the 1920s. There are also some actors whose names appear on casting call lists in existing studio records, who do not appear in the film; this includes Bobby Caldwell, William H. Davidson, Tom Dugan, and William Demarest.

The story deals with Chuckles, an old retired clown who recalls the heartache of circus life and has vowed to never deal with it again. Whenever one comes to town, he takes his son fishing. Happy, however, realizes his father's past prowess and secretly practices his acrobatic skills. Happy eventually runs away with the circus and his father struggles as to whether he is proud or ashamed. Happy starts out at the bottom, but eventually works his way up to becoming a performer. He becomes very fond of Alice (Patricia Ellis), an acrobat with the show. She works with her brother Frank (Gordon Westcott) who has a drinking problem. When Happy catches Frank drinking, he stops him as Alice walks in. To cover for Frank, Happy pretends it is he who is drinking, and guzzles the bottle down. This actually makes him drunk and he is fired from the circus. Returning to his father, he later reads of Alice's success and, encouraged by Chuckles, goes to win her back. He finds her arguing with Frank, who is drinking again. Happy punches Frank

---

37 Sawdust to have Realism. *Los Angeles Times*. February 13, 1934

and takes his place in the acrobatic act. He and Alice become a big hit, making Chuckles proud.

Joe E. Brown enjoyed one of his happiest experiences working on *Circus Clown* and recalling his roots in show business, dusting off a few old acrobatic routines. However, there was some trouble when Joe had to work closely with a trained lion in the film, getting quite close to the animal. According to the press:

> Joe E, Brown, wide-mouthed film comedian, exhibited a lacerated ear and nose today as mementoes of a one-sided encounter with a trained lion. All the sound effects of Joe's enormous mouth went Into an ear-splitting "ouch" when the beast lunged at him, tearing his nose and ear, and bringing blood. Brown was given emergency hospital treatment before resuming the picture. He then kept a safe distance between himself and the lion.[38]

This incident deals with Happy's friendship with Leo, a friendly lion with the circus, while Dynamite, another lion in the circus, is a more vicious animal. At one point, Happy is sleeping and the lion comes in and starts licking and tickling his feet, which awakens him. He thinks it is friendly Leo, and walks him back to his cage. He finds Leo's cage occupied, and realizes it is Dynamite.

There are several highlights in *Circus Clown*, especially scenes in which Joe E. Brown displays his remarkable athletic prowess. Early in the film, Happy becomes smitten with what he thinks is a female bareback rider, not realizing it is a man in a woman's costume playing a circus character. There are some good gags as the man, and several others, keep the ruse going as a joke on Happy.

In both roles of Happy and Chuckles, Joe has the opportunity to be both funny and dramatic, with Alice having a small child she is caring for (it is revealed as her brother's kid, but throughout the film he refers to her as Mommy). Happy's warm relationship with the child adds more depth to his character and mirrors, to some extent, his connection with his own father. At one point, the child is shown bouncing on a makeshift trampoline in emulation of his hero Happy, just like Happy did so in honor of his father. The pride

---

38 Movie Lion Lunges at Film Comedian. *Racine Journal Times*. February 16, 1934

of Happy's the father is shown in a seriocomic scene where Chuckles is watching his son's big acrobatic act with Alice. The scene is made amusing with a disgruntled audience member putting down Happy's performance, much to Chuckles' chagrin. The audience member is played by a young Ward Bond, who would eventually become a top level character actor and TV western star.

Circus Clown had yet to be released when an article on Joe E. Brown's next projects hit the press:

> Joe E. Brown will be back in about a month from his trip to the Orient. There have been rumors that he might go on the stage upon his return, but there Is little chance of this being accomplished. Brown has two pictures to make almost Immediately. One is *Six-Day Bike Race* and the other is *The Earthworm Tractor*. Joe will be making up for lost time at a great rate during the next few months, despite the fact that he still has one picture to be released, *The Circus Clown*.[39]

Upon returning home, Joe was put right to work on his next film, and was actively engaged with production of *The 6 Day Bike Rider* when *Circus Clown* was released.

Needing a hit after the disappointing *A Very Honorable Guy*, Joe and Warner Brothers were pleased when *Circus Clown* was a hit with both critics and moviegoers. The critic for *The Los Angeles Times* wrote:

> Life behind the scenes in a circus hold a perennial fascination for children and grown up alike. There is something about the relaxing clown, who forgets his funny business, his close association of the giant and the dwarf, and the child sleeping in his mother's wardrobe trunk, which intrigue the layman. This interest is again revealed in Joe E. Brown s production *Circus Clown*. Since Comedian Brown began his theatrical career in the sawdust medium and has been clowning on and off screen ever since, the role of Happy Howard, who runs awry to join a circus, is a natural for him. He appears more at home In the charac-

---

39 Two Films Await Comedian Brown. *Los Angeles Times*. May 19, 1934.

terization than in any previous one. in the opinion of this reviewer.

Circus Clown featured a deviation from the sort of character Brown had been playing in his movies prior to *A Very Honorable Guy*. In *Circus Clown*, his character is—for want of a better word—a pretty normal guy who possesses some great skills. He's not overly wacky or egotistical or boastful. In fact, most of his actions, such as pretending to drink to cover up for Alice's brother, are driven by very noble and selfless intentions. The story, even though it's primarily a comedy, feels more grounded in reality too. Nothing really happens that is overly fantastical, like in some of Brown's previous work.

Joe's benevolence was evident when a Newark, New Jersey theater planned a special screening of *Circus Clown* for children from an orphanage. The theater manager contacted Warner Brothers in hopes that Joe would send a recorded greeting of some sort. Joe got back to the theater manager personally and told him to allow the children to have all the popcorn, peanuts, and lemonade they wanted for free, and to send him the bill.

6 DAY BIKE RIDER

Directed by Lloyd Bacon
Screenplay: Earl Baldwin
Cinematography: Warren Lynch
Film Editing: George Amy

Cast:
Joe E. Brown, Maxine Doyle, Frank McHugh, Gordon Westcott, Arthur Aylesworth, Lottie Williams, Dorothy Christy, Lloyd Neal, William Granger, George Chandler, Luke Cosgrave, Dan Crimmins, Ben Hendricks jr, George Ovey, Clarence Wilson, Tammany Young, Charles Sellon, Ward Bond, Nora Cecil, Bill Elliot, Billy Dooley, Grace Hayle, John Quillan, Eddy Chandler, Frank Hagney, Steve Clark, Gertrude Hoffman, Ray Cooke, Selmer Jackson, Eddie Shubert, Tom Wilson, Matty Roubert, Kathrin Clare Ward, Frank Marlowe, Jack McHugh, Eugene Strong, Ralph Remley, Bruce Mitchell, Gus Leonard, Si Jenks, Billy Erwin, Robert Homans, Selmer Jackson.

Released October 20, 1934
Running time: 69 minutes
Warner Brothers
Black and White

During the 1930s, people amused themselves with a variety of endurance contests. Perhaps the most notable are the marathon dances that were depicted in Sydney Pollack's film *They Shoot Horses Don't They* (1969). Days-long bike races were something of a "thing" back then as well, and writer Earl Baldwin wrote up a story treatment about a confident nebbish who got around by bicycle and ended up competing in a marathon bike race as per the title. The story was accepted, so Baldwin wrote a screenplay. Baldwin's most recent screenplay used by Joe E. Brown was the atypical and ulti-

Joe in The 6 Day Bike Rider

mately less successful *A Very Honorable Guy*, so this time he created a script more akin to the comedian's talents. It was ready and waiting when Joe returned from the Orient, and was rushed into another production by Warner Brothers.

Joe plays Winfred Simpson a small town hick who runs the town's postal and telegraph office. Despite his limited status, he has an air of secure confidence which sometimes comes off in a conceited manner. Winfred is with his girl Phyllis (Maxine Doyle) when he is approached by Harry St Clair (Gordon Westcott), a handsome young man who is expecting a bicycle shipment and wants Winfred to open up after hours so he can get it. Winfred refuses at first but is eventually talked into it. It is a C.O.D. package and St Clair doesn't have the money, so he writes Winfred an IOU. Winfred is reluctant, but a telegram comes in that he has to deliver quickly, so he hastily accepts the terms. St Clair responds by giving him and Phyllis tickets to his upcoming trick bicycle show in town. While Winfred is away delivering the telegram, Harry walks Phyllis home. She is quite obviously attracted to him, which annoys Winifred.

Since Winifred goes everywhere by bicycle, he is quite adept at handling one, so he is vocally unimpressed by Harry's stunts when they attend the show. Harry then invites Winfred on stage. He accepts and while he is showing off with his own stunts, Harry sneaks into the audience and escorts an embarrassed Phyllis home. This causes a rift between an angry Phyllis and an offended Winfred, who leaves town and connects with Clinton Hemmings (Frank

McHugh) who gives him a ride. Clinton and Winfred enter a 6 man bike race to compete with Harry. They get jobs as bicycle messengers so they can practice. When Winfred is assigned to deliver a message to Harry, in town for the big race, he overhears a woman in the room and figures it is Phyllis so he bursts in and starts a fight. This causes him to get arrested and sent to jail, forcing Clinton to race alone, until he can somehow get out and make it to the track.

Warner Brothers studio was interested in getting Joe E. Brown into a movie quickly because the reaction to *A Very Honorable Guy* had been less appreciative than Joe's other movies, and they didn't want too much disruption of his momentum. Exhibitors acknowledged that the movie was not well liked by their audiences, but would state in their reports that any star could be forgiven for a misfire. Warner was a bit edgy about how *The Circus Clown* might be received. They wanted to hurriedly get a more typical Joe E. Brown vehicle in theaters.

With *6 Day Bike Rider*, Joe was able to call upon several established elements of his screen persona. First was his playing a generally confident, borderline conceited, character. He wasn't so much a braggart attempting to prove himself, Winfred was fixed and settled into his small town environment. However, when he and Phyllis break up, he mentions that he felt perhaps the town was too small for him, and he could make a difference in a bigger city. The fickleness of Phyllis is borne of small town innocence, as she doesn't realize she's being used by attractive Harry, who is actually a married man. The viewer admires Winfred's determination rather than being put off by his conceited naivete, especially when rival Harry is presented as so despicable.

It is interesting that when Phyllis tries to return to Winfred after she realizes her mistake in choosing Harry instead, Winfred won't take her back. He isn't mean, he just simply isn't about to accept an apology which is being made because of discovering the errors of her ways. Those errors were enough to turn off Winfred completely. It is not until Phyllis becomes instrumental in freeing Winfred from jail and allowing him to make it to the race that she is forgiven. By freeing him from jail, Winfred was able to see that

Joe and Maxine Doyle in The 6 Day Bike Rider

Phyllis really was sincere in her apology to him; it was more than just words.

The racing scenes are limited to the technology of the times, so the back projection that is utilized is forgiven for its visual limitation. That said, director Lloyd Bacon draws on his silent comedy roots and is able to present some truly exciting race scenes despite the use of back projection.

For authenticity, the film is filled with actual cyclists with experience in such competitions, not only for technical advisement, but to appear as extras in the racing scenes:

> When members of the sporting fraternity labeled a six day bike race a "whirl to nowhere," they probably little realized the significance of that term. However, significant as that phrase is in describing the 142 hour grind on a saucer track, the riders themselves have the satisfaction of know-

Promotional ad for The 6 Day Bike Rider

ing that in mileage covered they could have circumnavigated the globe many times had they pedaled in a straight path around the world at the equator. The professional riders appearing in Joe E. Brown's new First National comedy *6 Day Bike Rider* got their heads together during the production of the feature, and figured that the group of them had traveled in a distance equal to circumnavigating the world seven and one-half times, or a distance of slightly more than 179,325 miles. Leading the group in mileage covered and number of races was Reggie McNamara, the "Iron Man" of six day racing, who at 48 Is still one of the fastest competitive riders. McNamara. in his 30 years on the saucer track, has ridden in 108 races for a total of 130,000 miles, which gives him a circumnavigation of the globe more than five times. Reggie, however, has competed in many countries, these events taking him actually around the world twice. The oldest rider in six-day racing today, Reggie still holds many world records on the bicycle. His speed of one minute and forty-five seconds on the saucer track for a mile has never been touched. He likewise holds the five mile record at 9 minutes, 30 seconds the 10 mile at 18 minutes, 50 seconds, and the 25 mile at 51 minutes. Also appearing in Brown's comedy is Lew Rush of Victoria. Canada, who is considered one of the speediest riders today, and a rider with endless endurance. During the making of the picture, an unavoidable spill seriously Injured Rush and he was out of the picture during the last few days of shooting. The cream of six-day bike racing Is further represented in the lineup of the comedy. Among the other riders are Steve Wagner, a young German; Felix LaFenetre. who hails from France; Cecil "Rabbit" Yates from Chicago; Tony Shaller, also from the Windy City; Eddie Testa, teammate of McNamara; Frederick Schultz, another German rider; Bobbie Echeverrla, of Spanish descent; Geary May, a Canadian and winner with LaFenetre of a recent grind In Hollywood, Frankie Tarano, from Brooklyn; Sebastian Schmidt, a Hungarian; Neil Davidson, Los Angeles. This aggregation of many of the leading riders, all of whom are entertainers at heart, has given *6 Day Bike Rider* complete authenticity. The picture is a hilarious comedy in which Joe becomes the hero of a six-day bicycle race under the most amusing circumstances.[40]

---

40 Bike Racers Have Circled Globe Almost Eight Times. *The Times*. Sherveport, LA. November 27, 1934

Despite the professionalism, there were several injuries among the participants during the making of this movie. A significant accident occurred when the bike riders crashed into a cameraman filming them racing from a motorcycle

Joe E. Brown and Frank McHugh once again work well together. McHugh probably worked second best with Brown, after his fine work with James Cagney. Maxine Doyle is attractive and likeable as Phyllis, and Gordon Westcott is sufficiently oily as the handsome heavy. Westcott would likely have grown as an actor had he not died in a car crash about a year after this movie's release. Joe liked Westcott, who would appear again with him in *Bright Lights*, made shortly before he died.

There were several fun promotional events connected to *6 Day Bike Rider*. One theater in Provo, Utah held a bike race for kids where they would bike down a designated path and back to the theater. The first place winner received $2, second place was $1, and the next ten got free movie passes. It shows how inexpensive movie admissions were.

According to the press, plans for Joe E. Brown to next appear in *Earthworm Tractors* were put on hold:

> *Mollie and Me* will probably be the next picture for Joe E. Brown. He wasn't enthusiastic about *The Earth-Worm Tractor*, and it is a question whether that will be produced. The adapting of *Mollie and Me* is in the hands of Benny Rubin and Ben Markson.[41]

In fact, Joe had already appeared in a movie by the title *Molly and Me* in 1930 for the low budget Tiffany studios. The story was by Harry Durant, and the screenplay adaption was by Fredric and Fanny Hatton. The blurb above likely refers to Bert Kalmar and Harry Ruby's *Bright Lights*, which has a similar plot to *Molly and Me*, and did have Benny Rubin and Ben Markson working on the script.

However, before he embarked on *Bright Lights*, Joe E. Brown made his third and final baseball comedy, *Alibi Ike*.

---

41   Mollie and Me is Joe E. Brown's Next. *Los Angeles Times*. December 28, 1934

ALIBI IKE

Directed by Ray Enright
Screenplay: William Wister Haines from a story by Ring Lardner
Produced by Edward Chodorov
Cinematography: Arthur L. Todd
Film Editing: Thomas Pratt

Cast:
Joe E. Brown, Olivia de Havilland, Ruth Donnelly, Roscoe Karns, William Frawley, Eddie Shubert, Paul Harvey, Joe King, Joseph Crehan, G. Pat Collins, Spencer Charters, Gene Morgan, Wade Boteler, Frank Coghlan, jr, Louis Natheaux, Cliff Saum, Huey White, Eddy Chandler, Bill Elliot, Selmer Jackson, Milton Kibbee, Wilfred Lucas, Jack Norton, Jed Prouty, Frank Sully, Jim Thorpe, Fred "Snowflake" Toones, Herman Bell, Dick Cox, Cedric Durst, Ray French, Mike Gazella, Wally Hebert, Wally Hood, Don Hurst, Mead Jolley, Wes Kingdon, Lou Koupal, Jim Levy, Bob Meusel, Wally Rehg, George Riley, Frank Shellenback, Ed Wells, Phillip Sleeman, Adrian Rosley, Bruce Mitchell, Sam Hayes, Jack Cheatham, Pauline Brooks.

Released June 15, 1935
Running time: 72 minutes
Warner Brothers
Black and White

Press accounts as to Joe E. Brown's upcoming movies continued to mention *Mollie and Me*, which would become *Bright Lights*, as well as an intriguing production that never did get made:

> There are plenty of stories lined up for Joe E. Brown. He has three to do in the immediate future. They will probably be made in the following order: *Cops and Robbers*, by Walter

Trade ad for Alibi Ike

MacEwen, with Manuel Seff adaptation; then *Mollie and Me* and finally *Alibi Ike*, written by Ring Lardner. Joe Brown comedies have been a bit scarce for a time, but it looks as if the supply for the present year will be plentiful.

Walter MacEwan was producer Hal Wallis's assistant, and would not embark on being a filmmaker on his own for several years. *Cops and Robbers* never went beyond the initial planning stage. *Bright Lights* would be Joe's next film after *Alibi Ike*.

Olivia de Havilland and Joe in Alibi Ike

Concluding his baseball trilogy with the best of the three, Joe E. Brown is exceptional as the title character, who can never admit to what he's actually doing, no matter how inconsequential. His excuses are often outrageous, but because his talent is so exceptional, his manager and the rest of the team accept this sometimes annoying character trait. There is a lot of great humor that comes out of Farrell's inability to tell the truth about anything. And there's nothing malicious about his lies or the intent behind them, which allows Farrell to still be a likeable character.

The film's conflicts include not only practical jokes made by teammates to take advantage of his alibis, but also crooks who capture him and attempt to force Farrell to throw the game. He falls in love with Dolly, the sister of the team manager's wife, and his alibis cause a conflict which results in his losing a game due to distraction. The crooks believe Farrell threw the game for them, and send him money by messenger in an envelope he opens in front of the team manager and owner. When word gets to the crooks that he plans to win the next game despite their threats, they kidnap Farrell who is forced to escape and make it to the diamond in time.

Dolly is played by Olivia de Havilland, who was, at the time, a newcomer to movies. Olivia had been brought to Warner Brothers through Max Reinhardt who was to film his popular stage version of William Shakespeare's *A Midsummer Night's Dream* for the studio. Olivia as Hermia and Mickey Rooney as Puck were the only actors from the stage production to also be hired for the film. Warner Brothers signed her to a contract, and while *Midsummer* was in post-production, they quickly placed her in this Joe E. Brown comedy. Unfortunately, Ms. de Havilland felt that appearing in a movie with the nation's biggest comedy star was a comedown from the prestigious Shakespearean production, stating in a British Film Institute lecture in 1971:

"They did rather see me as an ingenue. And I was quite upset when they cast me immediately after in *Alibi Ike*." Nevertheless, she turns in an earnest performance. The irony: Joe E Brown is also in the film version of *A Midsummer Night's Dream*, and would receive the best notices among any of the actors.

William Frawley registers nicely as Cap, the baseball team's manager. With his gruff, comic presence, he is a good counterpart to the Farrell character. Frawley was a real life baseball fan, and when later playing his iconic Fred Mertz character on TV's *I Love Lucy*, he had it written in his contract that he did not have to work during the World Series if the New York Yankees were competing (the Yankees were in the World Series nearly every year the show was in production).

The cast is rounded out by wisecracking Ruth Donnelly, a 1930s Warner stalwart, as Cap's wife (and Dolly's sister), as well as several welcome character types playing Farrell's teammates, most notably Roscoe Karns, who gives Farrell the Alibi Ike nickname and often tries to call his bluff.

And while several actual baseball players of the period appear in cameo roles to add authenticity, bigger names had originally been sought:

> Hollywood's best baseball fan Joe E Brown has ideas for Ring Lardner's story *Alibi Ike*. Joe E wants to make it an epic of the diamond and he is asking Warner Brothers to get Babe Ruth and Ty Cobb to play. Cobb, it appears, is

Alibi Ike *was the third in Joe's baseball trilogy*

in San Francisco. Ruth will be more difficult to reach but telegrams are paging him. And just so *Alibi Ike* and baseball get a break together the picture will be rushed Into production so that it can be released with the opening of America's favorite outdoor sport.[42]

---

42 Ty Cobb and Babe Ruth May Take Part in Diamond Epic. The Sacramento Bee. Feb 7, 1935

Actual ball players who can be spotted in the movie include Guy Cantrell, Dick Cox, Cedric Durst, Mike Gazella, Wally Hood, Don Hurst, Smead Jolley, Lou Koupal, Bob Meusel, Wally Rehg, and Jim Thorpe.

Alibi Ike was originally a story by Ring Lardner that appeared in *The Saturday Evening Post* on July 31, 1915. Lardner based the character on Leonard "King" Cole, an actual ball player who had a record of 20-4 with the 1910 Chicago Cubs, the third best single season winning percentage (.833) for a Cub in the 20th century. Sadly, Cole died of lung cancer in 1916 at the age of only 29.

This is the first of Joe E. Brown's baseball films where the character is a ball player rather than someone who happens to be adept at the sport but either distracted or uninterested. Farrell understands his ability, is secure and boastful, but his alibis and passionate connection to the game set him apart from the characters Brown played in *Fireman Save My Child* and *Elmer The Great*. At one point Farrell tells crooks who want him to throw the game, "I wouldn't try to lose on purpose if my own mother was on the other team."

Unlike other comics of the era, Joe E. Brown was muscular and athletic, much like Buster Keaton. But while Keaton would play a character who got pushed around and battled back with his wits, Joe played characters who weren't afraid of physical altercation. In the scene where gangsters surround Farrell and force him to agree to throw the game, their leader, Lefty Crawford bends Farrell's left arm behind his back in a hammer lock and threatens to do the same to his pitching arm. Farrell only agrees to get out of the situation. He actually loses the game due to being distracted by a rift with Dolly. When Farrell is kidnapped, he beats up three of Lefty's henchman to escape.

Alibi Ike was Joe E. Brown's biggest hit to date, and was also well received by critics. Frank Nugent of *The New York Times* stated:

> Joe E. Brown, who is to Warners what Garbo is to Metro and Shirley Temple is to Fox, returns in a genuinely accusing little comedy patterned after one of Ring Lardner's most famous baseball stories—the abbreviated saga of the apologetic player known as Alibi Ike. Alibi Ike, you might remember, was the cornfed rookie from Sauk Centre who

came to the Cubs with a fast ball, a good batting eye and a roundabout excuse for everything. When he was tired, he wouldn't just come out and say so; he'd mention that he had gravel in his shoes and might as well give his feet a rest. And when his teammates asked him whether it was true that he had given an engagement ring to the manager's wife's sister, he wouldn't admit it; he said, instead, that the girl just sat at his table, and asked for the ring, and he was tired of the rock anyway, and he was kinda sorry for her and he didn't exactly know what he was getting into. All of which was overheard by the young woman in question and led to no end of complications. Out of such situations as these and a few others that William Wister Haines thought up to pad out the screenplay, Warners have fashioned a merry little film that will appeal first to the Brown enthusiasts, second to the Lardner disciples, third to the followers of the national sport and fourth to the rank and file of filmgoers who think there is nothing like a harmless comedy to brighten the dull moments of a hot Summer's day. And, with a clientele like that to draw from, there is no reason to wonder about Mr. Brown's Garboesque stature in the Frères Warner eyes. If you know Mr. Brown at all, you will appreciate how amply he fills the role of the alibiing rookie. From the moment he crashes the ball park—and crashes is the word—to the one when he breaks away from the crooked gamblers (one of Mr. Haines's improvisations) and reaches the playing field in his pajamas just in time to save the crucial game, he is a "yeeeooowing" success. Bringing up the rear guard of the cast, and doing it quite well, too, are Olivia de Havilland, a charming newcomer who will be seen next Fall in the role of Hermia in *A Midsummer Night's Dream*; William Frawley, Ruth Donnelly, Paul Harvey, Joseph King and a few other tried and true veterans.[43]

 Moviegoers, whose attendance at every Joe E. Brown release resulted in his being one of the biggest stars in movies, flocked to

---

43 Alibi Ike review. *The New York Times*. July 17, 1935

see this latest offering. In Philadelphia where there was a real slump in movie theater attendance during the week before the Fourth of July, *Alibi Ike* was the only movie in the city to draw a profit. During a heat wave in Chicago, *Alibi Ike* was the best draw in the loop.

Some of the more interesting promotional idea from exhibitors included a theater owner in Texas that set up a Joe E. Brown carnival game to interest potential patrons. A five foot tall replica of Joe E. Brown's head was displayed with his already large mouth made into a large opening through which ticket buyers were invited to throw baseballs. A Pennsylvania theater invited local ball players to appear at *Alibi Ike* screenings and talk to kids about baseball.

Joe E. Brown was still not interested in filming *Earthworm Tractors* based on other stories that had appeared in *The Saturday Evening Post* about the enterprising Alexander Botts. However, after completing *Alibi Ike*, Joe was ready to do the heavily promoted *Mollie and Me*, a showbiz story that would be released as *Bright Lights*. Joe was especially attracted to this story because his character had more depth than just being a comic role -- something that worked well for him in *Circus Clown*, but not so well in *A Very Honorable Guy*. However, when *Bright Lights* became another big hit, Joe E. Brown's agent started considering other possibilities for his star.

BRIGHT LIGHTS

Directed by Busby Berkeley
Screenplay: Bert Kalmer and Harry Ruby, adapted by Ben Markson and Benny Rubin from a story by Lois Leeson.
Produced by Michael Curtiz
Cinematography: Sid Hickox
Film Editing: Bert L'Orle

Songs
She Was an Acrobat's Daughter
Lyrics by Bert Kalmar
Music by Harry Ruby

I'm All for You
Music by Allie Wrubel

You're an Eyeful of Heaven
Music by Allie Wrubel
Lyrics by Mort Dixon

Powder My Back
Music by Allie Wrubel
Lyrics by Mort Dixon

Nobody Cares If I'm Blue
Music by Harry Akst
Lyrics by Grant Clarke

Cast:
Joe E. Brown, Ann Dvorak, Patricia Ellis, William Gargan, Joseph Cawthorn, Henry O'Neill, Arthur Treacher, Gordon Westcott, Joseph Crehan, William Demarest, Irving Bacon, William B. Davidson, Howard Hickman, Eddie Larkin, June Travis, Glen Cavender, Bill Elliot, Sam Harris, Tom Kennedy, Gene Morgan, Milton Kibbee, Paul Panzer, Harry Seymour, George Gruhl, Charles Kaley, Clarence Wilson, Phil Ryley, Clifton Young,

August Tollaire, Victoria Vinton, Sam Ash, Jack Wise, Virginia Dabney, Sammy Blum, Carl Leviness, Harold Miller, Ruth Moody, The Maxellos

Released July 27, 1935
Running time: 82 minutes
Warner Brothers
Black and White

Bright Lights went into production immediately after Joe E. Brown finished work on *Alibi Ike*. Both *The Circus Clown* and *The 6 Day Bike Rider* were achieving box office success in theaters, and Brown was eager to expand upon his comic persona. He had already shot the uncharacteristic Shakespeare film *A Midsummer Night's Dream* which remained in post-production, but that was a challenge he didn't seek. However his success with the more layered character in *Circus Clown*, with a script that went beyond comic gags, showed the studio that Brown would be accepted by moviegoers as an actor who did comedy, and did not have to limit himself as a bombastic comedy presence. The fact that the offbeat *A Very Honorable Guy* had flopped turned out to be an aberration. *Bright Lights* showed audiences another side of Joe E. Brown the actor, and became a smash hit.

Joe E. Brown plays Joe Wilson, a top banana in Burlesque who is so successful in an act with his wife Fay (Ann Dvorak) that he is courted by Broadway producers. She sings and he plays a comic drunk who heckles her from the rafters. He also sings, dances, and does acrobatics. It is his enormous talent that the producers want. They insist he be paired with noted heiress Clare Whitmore (Patricia Ellis), because her name is "box office." Claire is the sort of entitled rich girl who engages in different experiences for her own enjoyment, and because she is now interested in theatrical work, the Broadway producers want to capitalize on her involvement. Joe is ready to quit, but Fay talks him into staying. With Fay remaining on the Burlesque circuit and Joe in New York on Broadway, circumstances result in the happily married man becoming smitten by Claire, who starts a romance with him. Things get so extreme that Joe sends a letter to Fay indicating he has fallen for someone

Newspaper ad for Bright Lights

else. However, when he walks in and finds Claire embracing producer Dan Wheeler (William Gargan), he is taken aback. When they announce their engagement he is shocked. He races to stop the letter to Fay, but is too late. Fay reads it just before going out on stage and tearfully goes into her act. Joe suddenly appears doing his drunk act and they go into their established routine like old times.

Joe E. Brown's performance in *Bright Lights* is a tour de force, drawing on his Burlesque roots and allowing him to exhibit several areas of his talent. He pulled out a lot of his routines from the vaudeville years, including an act for which he was best known before he started making movies. Wanda Hale in *The New York Daily News* stated:

> Joe E. Brown's renowned monologue concerning the "itsy-bitsy mouse and the great bwig pussy-tat" makes its public debut in *Bright Lights*. Joe (enters) his drunken rodent in competition with Mickey Mouse. When the big-mouthed Mr, Brown is not doing his monologue, he is picking them up and laying them down in happy emulation of Fred Astaire or perching precariously from theatre boxes like a fly gone berserk.

Brown engages in eccentric dances, backflips, bounces back from the orchestra pit (a hidden trampoline is used for that gag), and performs acrobatic routines with The Maxellos.

The heckling scenes, with a drunken Joe stumbling and fumbling up in the private balcony area, while Fay feeds him straight lines, is an age old vaudeville routine that continued to be used as late as the 1950s nightclub era by Dean Martin and Jerry Lewis (and is seen in their 1953 movie release *The Stooge*).

Joe: What's going on behind the curtain

Fay: Not a thing

Joe: Well take it up because there's nothing going on in front of it!

Fay: You ought be ashamed. I'm trying to sing!

Joe: If you're trying to sing, then you are the one that should be ashamed!

Joe punctuates his lines by drunkenly pretending to lose balance and almost fall into the audience, causing their thrill as well as their laughter.

Joe revisited his theater roots in Bright Lights *with Ann Dvorak*

While Joe E. Brown's skill as a dancer, singer, and acrobat is notable, his work as an actor playing a character has the most strength. Brown explores well past the parameters of his previous performances. Joe Wilson is not only a man of top skill, he is filled with enthusiasm and genuine affection for his wife. Fay is more than a performing partner; their early scenes of playfully cracking wise with each other, and responding physically with snuggling affection show a real, solid connection. This is further borne out when Joe

Joe is flanked by Ann Dvorak and Patricia Ellis in Bright Lights

is ready to give up his Broadway dream in loyalty to her. But her loyalty overrides his.

It is surprising that Joe responds to the romantic whims of Claire, as his early scenes with Fay show a genuine affection. But the point of the narrative is that Joe's Burlesque roots have not quite prepared him for the wealthy frivolity of an heiress who flits among men she finds interesting. Joe succumbs to the situation.

The conclusion is especially effective. Audiences of the period would not have been very forgiving of Joe's character if he actually did leave Fay for Claire, but the way the narrative is structured, it is shown as a stupid distraction for which he is obviously ashamed. Claire comes off as haughty and frivolous. Fay is very genuine. Both women are as attractive as each other.

It is also interesting that, along with being a comic, Joe E. Brown is something of a romantic lead here, however tenuous. While he has been connected to pretty girls in most of his movies, his rather blatant appearance makes these connections more comically based. In *Bright Lights* he is more seriously involved, being married and also succumbing to a distracting affair. It is another example of adding a layer to his established screen persona. This movie proves that Brown is capable of handling more dramatic fare if he so chooses. It also kind of follows a similar premise of some of his previous films—a guy whose talent plucks him from his natural environment and places him in a new one where he is a bit of a fish out of water—but it manages to strike a very different tone and still be successful.

Patricia Ellis had worked well with Joe E. Brown in *Elmer the Great* and *Circus Clown*. This is the only time that Ann Dvorak worked with Brown, but she did have a background in musical theater, and her first couple of years in movies were spent as part of the chorus. Dvorak had made an impact in Howard Hawks' *Scarface* (1932) and was thereafter hired by Warner Brothers. In rapid succession, Dvorak scored in such Warner films as *The Crowd Roars* (1932), *The Strange Love of Molly Louvain* (1932), *Three on a Match* (1932). When she appeared in *Bright Lights*, Dvorak had just finished work in one of her best films, *G-Men* (1935), opposite James Cagney. Director Busby Berkeley was the perfect filmmaker for this movie, having helmed Warner musicals like *42nd Street* (1932) and *Footlight Parade* (1933) to great success. *Bright Lights* is an interesting project for Berkeley, especially at this time in his career. The movie doesn't have any big flashy music numbers like his other films. But it shows that even for a movie set on a bit of a smaller scale, he was still a very adept director.

The response to *Bright Lights* was very positive, with critics proclaiming that Joe E. Brown's comedies were no longer for the children and family trade in rural cities, but could also extend to more sophisticated moviegoers in the big cities. Meanwhile, exhibitors wrote to the trades that *Bright Lights* was extremely well received by moviegoers:

> "Joe E. Brown seems as if he enjoyed every minute while making it. I hope, Joe, you can give us something nearly as good without waiting too long"

> "They don't come any better than this."

> "Joe E. Brown is my best bet. This is his best picture. It did extra business."

"We thought this was the best picture Joe E. Brown has ever made. He is the best actor on screen in my estimations. His pictures never fail to draw and please."

Along with being one of Joe E. Brown's best-received films at every level, it was also one of his biggest hits at the box office.

The year 1935 was a difficult one for the movie industry. The tax rolls dropped for all of the stars in Hollywood except two: Joe E. Brown and Joan Crawford. While most stars' films made less than the year previous, Joe's net worth more than doubled. Joe's agent, Mike Levee, had already been considering a better situation for a star of Joe E. Brown's magnitude. He was one of the most popular box office stars on the Warner Brothers lot, and one of its highest paid. Brown wondered if his current stardom could net a better financial deal elsewhere.

Bright Lights was made so quickly after *Alibi Ike*, the two films were released only about a month apart. So, Joe E. Brown had a sports comedy for the family trade, and a more serious musical comedy with some dramatic elements playing in the bigger cities for more sophisticated trade. The success of these films continued his box office status.

By the Fall of 1935, *A Midsummer Night's Dream* was ready for release, and although Joe E. Brown was reluctant to explore his ability so far beyond his wheelhouse and venture into Shakespeare, his became one of the most enjoyable performances in the movie.

A MIDSUMMER NIGHT'S DREAM

Director: William Dieterle, Max Reinhardt
Screenplay: by William Shakespeare. Arranged for the screen by Charles Kenyon and Mary C. McCall, jr.
Producer: Henry Blanke
Executive Producers: Hal Wallis, Jack Warner
Cinematography: Hal Mohr
Editing: Ralph Dawson
Makeup: Perc Westmore, Clay Campbell, Charles Gemora

The Athenian Court
Ian Hunter as Theseus, Duke of Athens
Verree Teasdale as Hippolyta, Queen of the Amazons, betrothed to Theseus
Hobart Cavanaugh as Philostrate, Master of Revels to Theseus
Dick Powell as Lysander, In love with Hermia
Ross Alexander as Demetrius, In love with Hermia
Olivia de Havilland as Hermia, In love with Lysander
Jean Muir as Helena, In love with Demetrius
Grant Mitchell as Egeus, Father to Hermia

The Players
Frank McHugh as Quince, the Carpenter
Dewey Robinson as Snug, the Joiner
James Cagney as Bottom, the Weaver
Joe E. Brown as Flute, the Bellows-mender
Hugh Herbert as Snout, the Tinker
Otis Harlan as Starveling, the Tailor
Arthur Treacher as Epilogue

The Fairies
Victor Jory as Oberon, King of the Fairies
Anita Louise as Titania, Queen of the Fairies

Nini Theilade as Fairie, Attending Titania
Mickey Rooney as Puck or Robin Goodfellow, a Fairy
Katherine Frey as Pease-Blossom
Helen Westcott as Cobweb
Fred Sale as Moth
Billy Barty as Mustard-Seed

Soundtrack:
Scottish Symphony"
Music by Felix Mendelssohn-Bartholdy
Adapted by Erich Wolfgang Korngold

Over Hill, Over Dale, Through Bush, Through Brier
Music by Felix Mendelssohn-Bartholdy
Words by William Shakespeare
Adapted and arranged by Erich Wolfgang Korngold from Mendelssohn's "Neue Liebe"

Spinning Song
Music by Felix Mendelssohn-Bartholdy
Adapted by Erich Wolfgang Korngold

Philomel
Music by Felix Mendelssohn-Bartholdy
Words by William Shakespeare

Cradle Song
from "Songs Without Words", Op. 67, No. 6
Music by Felix Mendelssohn-Bartholdy

Kinderstucke (Pieces for Children) no.1: Allegro non troppo"
Music by Felix Mendelssohn-Bartholdy
Lyrics are by William Shakespeare

Lullaby
Music by Felix Mendelssohn-Bartholdy
Words by William Shakespeare
Adapted by Erich Wolfgang Korngold

Hand In Hand With Fairy Grace
Music by Felix Mendelssohn-Bartholdy
Words by William Shakespeare

The ballet sequences featuring the fairies were choreographed by Bronislava Nijinska.

Released October 30, 1935
Running time: 133 minutes (142 minutes with overture and exit music)
Black and White

This adaption of Shakespeare features many actors who had never performed in one of the bard's works before and never would again, including Joe E Brown. In fact, in a book covering Joe E. Brown's films, there is a temptation to relegate *A Midsummer Night's Dream* to supporting role status and give it scant attention within another chapter as a mere curio. But, over time, this film has been rerun, put on home video, and available through streaming. And, despite the incongruity, Joe E. Brown's work does stand out.

Max Reinhardt was an important stage director in his native Germany, and was in the process of resuming his career after fleeing to America to escape Nazi rule. He staged *A Midsummer Night's Dream* at the Hollywood Bowl in September of 1934. The Program Designer/Annotator for Los Angeles Philharmonic, John Mangum recalled:

> It was spectacular production. The shell was removed and replaced by a 'forest' planted in tons of dirt hauled in especially for the event, and a trestle was constructed from the hills to the stage for the wedding procession between Acts IV and V. Reinhardt's son Gottfried later recalled, 'He worked out a torch parade for the last act, stepping to Mendelssohn's Wedding March, from the heights of the Hollywood Hills to the bottom of the valley.... It did not concern him that in Southern California's tinder-dry vegetation, that constituted a fire hazard of the first order.'" [44]

Despite Max Reinhardt's worldwide prominence, Warner Brothers was taking a real chance when choosing to do a film version in 1935. Six years earlier, Douglas Fairbanks and Mary Pickford had

---

44 Mangum, John. "A Midsummer Night's Dream" (complete): Felix Mendelssohn. www.hollywoodbowl.com.

produced a film version of Shakespeare's *The Taming of the Shrew* and it was a box office flop. As a result, movies based on Shakespeare's plays were still considered box office poison. The fact that Warner Brothers wanted to fill the cast with their own contracted stars was also a gamble in that most of them didn't have any experience with the Bard's works. The only actors hired from the Hollywood Bowl performance to appear in the film were Mickey Rooney and Olivia de Havilland, the latter of course having also done a movie with Joe E. Brown while *A Midsummer Night's Dream* was in post-production.

In his autobiography *Laughter is a Wonderful Thing*, Brown recalled, "The only Shakespeare I knew played for Notre Dame, but I didn't know he could act!" But since Warner Brothers had invested a lot of money to bring in Max Reinhardt and film the play, their decision to fill the cast with the popular names on their roster seemed to make good business sense.

Warner Brothers planted publicity stories in most of the major newspapers while the movie was in production. As early as February, a syndicated story indicated:

> Rarely has the curiosity of fans been so aroused over any motion picture as over *A Midsummer Night's Dream*. It is interesting to learn that Warners have decided to give the Max Reinhardt production, which has made moviegoers Shakespeare-conscious, an international premiere on October 15. *A Midsummer Night's Dream* with James Cagney, Dick Powell, Joe E. Brown, Jean Muir, Olivia de Haviland, Anita Louise and all the other stars, will be shown in New York, Washington, London, Paris, Buenos Aires and Vienna. After that, it will be road-showed in one city at a time. We can check another history-making event to the credit of Warner Brothers[45]

And during the summer post production, after Joe E. Brown had appeared in two other movies prior to this one's release, it was

---

45   Syndicated press release obtained from *The San Francisco Examiner*, July 2, 1935 issue

teased that perhaps a stage version with the film stars was being considered:

> Now that they've learned their parts, some of the members of *A Midsummer Night's Dream* cast want to remember them for a while, and possibly even indefinitely. It appears that they are forming an alumni association to perpetuate the giving of the production, and, as a token of their esteem lor Max Reinhardt. If the plan is carried out, a stage presentation of the Shakespearean comedy will be given annually. Leaders in the movement are James Cagney, Joe E. Brown and Dick Powell, They are planning a regular organization, the members of which will include the entire cast and technical crew. Actually If they played in the comedy on the stage they would have more lines to learn than will be heard from the screen in the finished version of *A Midsummer Night's Dream*.

No such stage production occurred, much less an annual event, and it is likely this was merely studio ballyhoo.

Although it was a gamble, it paid off for the studio. *A Midsummer Night's Dream* was a big hit, with Joe E. Brown and James Cagney receiving the bulk of the good press in the movie reviews. Cagney and Brown appeared in several scenes together, causing *The New York Times* to state in their review: "Joe E. Brown as Flute the Bellows-mender gives the best performance in the show. It is a privilege to roar with laughter when he is rehearsing for the rude masque or playing the timid Thisbe to James Cagney's Pyramus." Joe is very funny in *A Midsummer Night's Dream*, even though it isn't necessarily his normal brand of humor. The effeminate mannerisms and high-pitched voice he puts on could have been too over-the-top, but end up being just amusing enough.

An article in the *San Francisco Examiner* incorrectly claimed that Joe E. Brown sought out the role in the Shakespearian film:

> From the day Joe E. Brown entered pictures he has been a star. He has starred in fifteen Warner Bros, productions and in the sixteenth was content with being one of the cast of other stars. In *A Midsummer Night's Dream*, he

Joe and James Cagney hold their own despite being out of their element in the screen version of Shakespeare's A Midsummer Night's Dream

plays the part of Flute. This is by no means the leading part; it is however, an important piece in the intricate pattern Shakespeare has woven, Brown felt the importance of the production was the biggest thing of its kind ever made, coupled with the opportunity to work with Max Reinhardt. It was a case where the artist dominated the man.[46]

Joe E. Brown would later state in his autobiography: "The Bard's words have been spoken better, but never bigger or louder! It was one of the most successful pictures I did."

Something perhaps more significant than appearing in a successful screen adaption of a Shakespeare play was going on in Joe

---

46 Joe E. Brown Plays for Art. *The San Francisco Examiner.* November 20, 1935

E. Brown's life. His agent, Mike Levee, had made a deal with independent producer David Loew for Joe to appear in independent productions and increase his per-film salary to $100,000 per picture. Loew's father was Marcus Loew, the Metro in Metro-Goldwyn-Mayer when the three merged to form MGM. Marcus Loew also was president of a theater chain, and when he died in 1927, David was in charge of the theater chain's Board of Directors. David wanted to begin a career as a Hollywood producer and in 1935 resigned from Loew's Inc. Naturally, he jumped at the chance of signing a top star like Joe E. Brown.

Joe was currently the highest paid actor on the Warner Brothers lot, and among the biggest stars in movies, so securing a better paying deal was not difficult. Joe signed with David Loew before the end of 1935, then proceeded to finish off the final year in his Warner Brothers contract. Ironically, 1936 turned out to be Joe E. Brown's most successful year in movies.

SONS O' GUNS

Directed by Lloyd Bacon
Screenplay: Jerry Wald and Julius Epstein from the play by Fred Thompson and Jack Donahue.
Produced by Hal Wallis
Cinematography: Sol Polito
Film Editing: James Gibbon

Songs:
For a Buck and a Quarter a Day
Music by Harry Warren
Lyrics by Al Dubin

In the Arms of an Army Man
Music by Harry Warren
Lyrics by Al Dubin
Sung by Wini Shaw

Over Here
Music by J. Fred Coots
Lyrics by Benny Davis and Arthur Swanstrom
Sung by Joe E. Brown and chorus

Cast:
Joe E. Brown, Joan Blondell, Beverly Roberts, Eric Blore, Craig Reynolds, Winifred Shaw, Joseph King, Robert Barrat, G.P. Huntley, Frank Mitchell, Bert Roach, David Worth, Hans Joby, Michael Mark, Otto Fries, Mischa Auer, Emmett Vogan, Robert Adair, Pat Flaherty, Henry Otho, Sol Gross, Bill Dagwell, James Eagles, Leo Sulky, Don Turner, Max Wagner, Jack Wise, Milton Kibbee, Allen Matthews, Denny Sullivan, Eddie Shubert, Olaf Hytten.

Released May 30, 1936
Running time: 82 minutes
Warner Brothers
Black and White

The release of *A Midsummer Night's Dream*, which had been filmed earlier, gave Warner Brothers time to assess the box office performance of *Bright Lights*. When that film was a hit with moviegoers and critics, it was decided that Joe finally get to work on another musical comedy with a few opportunities for pathos.

There was a great deal of anticipation regarding *Sons O' Guns*, a former stage musical featuring Al Jolson. Robin Coons offered some backstory about the project in the press:

> Joe E Brown probably was nowhere near Palm Springs the desert resort when the contract that led to his present starring vehicle was signed. *Sons O'Guns* after four years of hanging fire as a film production is underway at last. Behind it is one of those stories that make the movie lots both unbelievable and fascinating. Al Jolson and Joe Schenck, the producer, were talking things over one sunny day at Palm Springs and they agreed that a Jolson picture under Schenck auspices would be a good idea, Al was then the original Warner talkie star but the association was wearing thin, He thereupon, without ado, signed a contract with Schenck on the only stationery handy— a paper bag. It was an empty paper bag and the lack of content was to prove sadly symbolic. Schenck purchased the Broadway musical *Sons o' Guns* as a Jolson vehicle but the screen treatment did not jell. Al's salary did however, and in full. After a year of waiting for something to happen Jolson left for the east. But Jolson had faith in *Sons o' Guns* and bought it from Schenck. Back at Warner's he found a star eager for it — none other than Joe E Brown who was nowhere near Palm Springs when it all began.[47]

Columnist Louella Parsons was one of the more notable journalists who also gave the production some advance publicity.

> I should not be surprised if Warner Brothers made a top-notch screen musical comedy out of *Sons o' Guns*. This musical has been kicking around Hollywood longer than any other piece of property Joseph Schenck bought it at the height of the success as a stage musical -comedy

---
47 Coons, Robin. Empty Paper Bag. *San Pedro News-Pilot*. January 13, 1936

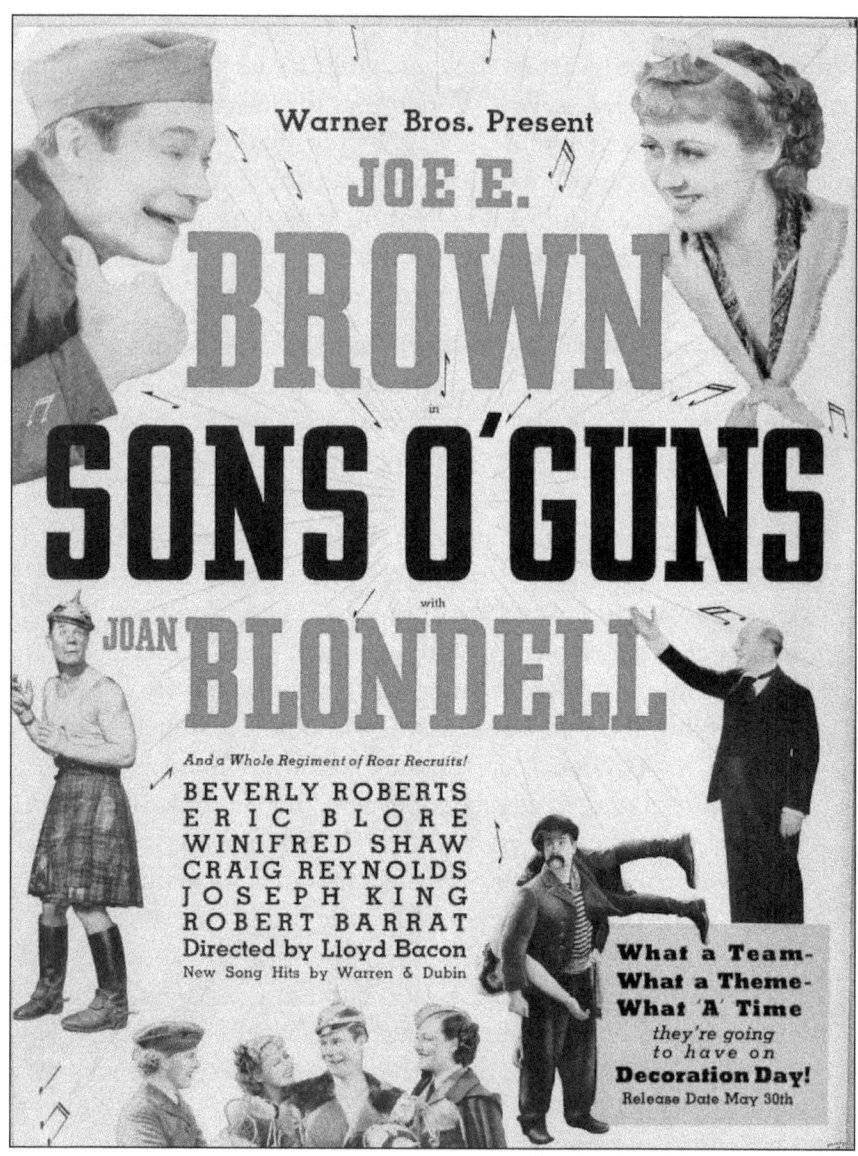

Trade ad for Sons O' Guns

intending it first for Lili Damita who had starred in the stage play. Always something happened to interfere with the production until four years passed. Jack Warner has purchased the film rights and will star Joe E Brown who made his biggest success in years in *Bright Lights* a musical. Perhaps Lili Damita will play opposite him.[48]

However, it was not Lili Damita but Warners contract player Joan Blondell who played the role of the French girl in the Joe E. Brown movie version.

Joe E. Brown plays Jimmy Canfield, a musical performer during World War One who is a true pacifist at every level and refuses to join the war effort. As a result, his girlfriend won't marry him because her father, a General, disapproves. Bernice, an old flame shows up and in order to evade her, Jimmy pretends to be enlisting and joins a group of marching soldiers while wearing a stage costume uniform. He ends up actually in the Army, where he discovers his effete valet (Eric Blore) is now his no-nonsense Sergeant. He meets Yvonne, a French girl, and becomes smitten with her, but she is jealous of both Mary and Bernice who come to the military camp at different times – Mary to see her father, and Bernice to appear in a company show. While staying at Yvonne's inn, where she lives with her stepfather, Jimmy can't sleep due to the noise of some carrier pigeons, so he opens a window and allows them to fly away. Turns out Yvonne's stepdad is a spy and those pigeons are trained to bring information to the enemy. Jimmy is arrested and destined to be shot, but he manages to steal an officer's uniform and escapes, only to end up in a trench with orders to capture a German machine gun. When a shell explodes and blows away his uniform, Jimmy grabs a convenient helmet and the enemy gunners believe he is one of their officers when he dons an officer's coat and orders a retreat. Jimmy captures a regimen of German soldiers, but because he is still wearing the enemy attire, he is considered a spy by the allies. He is thrown into the guardhouse again but when he is taken out, he is not executed, but decorated, as the real truth of his heroism has been discovered.

Because it was made between the wars, the argument of patriotism vs. pacifism wasn't something at the forefront of the culture when *Sons O' Guns* was initially released. This was simply a comic conflict within the narrative, while the military setting allows for

---

48 Parsons, Louella. Joe E. Brown To Star in Musical Film. *The Sacramento Bee.* November 21, 1935

a few vaudeville gags that would later be utilized by the likes of Abbott and Costello. And due to the success of *Bright Lights*, this film is another tour de force for Brown, who is able to sing, dance, play comedy, and do pathos.

There are many very funny moments in *Sons O' Guns*. The effete valet/Sergeant is delightful when demonstrating self-defense methods that render the athletic Jimmy helpless. Jimmy jealously responding to a couple of prisoners enjoying anything they want to eat while he must settle for guardhouse rations, until he realizes it is their last meal before execution. Sharing a bottle of liquor with an officer guard, and getting him so drunk, Jimmy is able to steal his uniform and escape. An underwear-clad Jimmy, after a shell has blown away his uniform, jumping up and down to see over the edge of the trench in which he's hiding. And hundreds of German soldiers being inspired by Jimmy's pacifism and all deciding to surrender, en masse.

It is particularly impressive when Jimmy is first confronted for releasing the pigeons and being told he is being arrested. He jumps from a window, slides down a roof, and flips into a pile of hay, before getting up and running to join his unit. It is a remarkable piece of comic acrobatics, especially when one realizes Joe E. Brown was past 40 when he made this movie.

Joan Blondell is a lot of fun as the French Yvonne, calling on her natural comic talents, and engaging in some delightful musical numbers with Joe. Only one of the songs, "Over Here," is from the original stage show. The other numbers were composed for this movie. Luppee Lupien, a French-Canadian actress, coached Blondell with her French accent.

Even though 1936 was a lame duck year at Warners for Joe E. Brown, as he had already signed to go with producer David Loew when his contract with the studio lapsed, the premiere for *Sons O' Guns* was quite an event:

> The world premiere of Joe E. Brown's new Warner Bros, starring picture, *Sons O' Guns*, will be a gala affair on Wednesday evening at the New York Strand Theatre, with many celebrities of stage, screen and radio, as well as officers of the Army and Navy and patriotic organizations,

Joe explains his friendship with Beverly Roberts to a jealous Joan Blondell in Sons O' Guns

in attendance. *Sons O' Guns* is based on the famous musical comedy of several seasons ago.[49]

Sons O' Guns was another hit for Joe E. Brown, with both children and adults enjoying his antics and the story.

Warner Brothers had long wanted Joe E. Brown to play Alexander Botts, a popular Saturday Evening Post character, but Brown wasn't attracted to the project and the idea was shelved. Now that the comedian was finishing up his contract at the studio, it was decided that he would, indeed, make *Earthworm Tractors* based on the Botts character. It turned out to be another of Joe's most enjoyable films.

---

49 Gala Opening Set For Sons O' Guns. *Brooklyn Times Union*. May 10, 1936.

EARTHWORM TRACTORS

Directed by Ray Enright
Screenplay: Richard Macaulay, Joe Traub, and Hugh Cummings from the stories by William Hazlett Upson
Produced by Samuel Bischoff
Cinematography: Arthur Todd
Film Editing: Doug Gould

Cast:
Joe E. Brown, June Travis, Guy Kibbee, Dick Foran, Carol Hughes, Gene Lockhart, Olin Howland, Joseph Crehan, Rosalind Marquis, Charles C. Wilson, William B Davidson, Irving Bacon, Stuart Holmes, Harry Depp, Jack Wise, Spec O'Donnell, Jerry Fletcher, Henry Hall, Tom Wilson, John J. Richardson, Milton Kibbee, Victoria Vinton, Henry Otho, Harvey Perry, Russ Powell.

Released July 24, 1936
Running time: 69 minutes
Warner Brothers
Black and White

Joe E. Brown's misgivings about playing a screen version of short story character Alexander Botts was because he felt it was all wrong for his character. So he kept avoiding the project until finally, during his lame duck year with Warner Brothers, he accepted the role to help fulfill the final throes of his contract. However, changes were made to transform the Botts character into more like the type of role Joe E. Brown had become noted for playing, much to the chagrin of original author William Hazlett Upson. What we end up with is a pretty typical Joe E. Brown comedy in which he, as the central character, chases big ideas, fails often, but finally triumphs.

There are general similarities to the Botts character and the Joe E. Brown screen persona. Botts is a mechanic who prides himself as

Earthworm Tractors *was a movie Joe didn't want to do, but it turned out to be a success*

a super salesman, and takes on the selling of the tractors he works on, failing and getting fired, and rehired, along the way. That is a basic trajectory of the Joe E. Brown comic formula as well. But where Botts is hard working and determined, Joe's characters are usually lovable boasters who back up their talent. In this case, Joe is boasting, but it takes some time for him to acquire the skill, and the luck, to succeed.

As Alexander Botts, Joe is a small town small timer who is making mere pocket change peddling a cheap novelty. His sweetheart Sally (Carol Hughes) wants him to make good, and her father (Olin Howard) doesn't want him anywhere near the house until he's successful. Meanwhile, Botts has a rival for Sally's attention, Emmett (Dick Foran), who scoffs at the idea of Botts being a success. Botts appears to confuse the term "making it big" with selling items that are large in size, so he writes a boastful letter to the Earthworm Tractor company and, through a series of circumstances, ends up being hired. The company head (Charles Wilson), hopes this ambitious newcomer can close a deal with the difficult Mr. Jackson. On his way to meet the client, Botts sees Mabel (June Travis) who's car is stuck in the mud, so he helps her. She suggests that Botts try to sell a tractor to her father, Sam (Guy Kibbee), indicating that he is a very tough customer. Sam's last name is Johnson, and Botts mistakes the name with Jackson the client he's been assigned to see. As part of his pitch, Botts has Sam take a demonstration ride in the tractor, but because he knows nothing about the vehicle, he ends up on a relentless path of destruction. Coincidentally, Jackson, the actual client, has viewed how powerful the tractor is, and agrees to purchase several. Botts becomes attracted to Mabel, but remains true to Sally. However, when he goes back home a success, he discovers Sally has married Emmett. He returns to Mabel, who is offended that she is second choice. After another wild tractor ride with Botts and Sam Johnson, an explosion cures the old man's hearing and Botts not only wins Mabel's hand, he sells another fleet of tractors to Sam.

Original author William Hazlett Upson had worked for the Caterpillar tractor company and based his Alexander Botts stories on his own experiences. And while the title is a play on the Caterpillar name, that company donated some of its own tractors to use during filming and allowed a second unit to film at their headquarters in East Peoria, Illinois. Caterpillar Co. spent around $250,000 on ads and brochures featuring Joe E. Brown with their tractors, which not only supported the film, but helped promote their business.

Joe E. Brown recalled in an interview at the time that he had been preparing to play a salesman for most of his adult life, because he had been the target of salesmen.

> I don't know why salesmen regard me as the perfect specimen of a man sadly lacking that quality which business men call sales resistance. They do, though, and I have gone through life buying things I didn't need with money I didn't have to store away in closets packed with other similar things I didn't want. My home out here looks like a section of the British Museum, and I usually have to move. each year or so, in order to lose some of the things which have cluttered up the house. We have to lose the stuff. It couldn't be given away. Take for instance, a gad-

get I have which takes up all the space in a spare room which is badly needed for other purposes. It was sold to me by a young man with the perseverance of a beaver and a hat that was three sizes too big for him. I think I finally bought the thing on account of the hat. I wanted to see him take it off when he came into the house. Anyway, the boy started off by saying he wanted to sell me a grand piano. I told him I had one that another man had sold me the week before. He immediately became suspicious. Did it have an adjustable wheel-base with radio attachment he asked. No, but It did have a convertible wash stand with comfortable space for three cakes of soap, I answered. I thought I had him there. He cried in a delighted manner, he sold you a 1934 model. It probably didn't even have the knee-action keyboard. I admitted sadly that It didn't. Well, he answered as he pulled out his order blank, this one has. It's also got streamlined legs and plays 46 records without stopping. The records are extra, how many do you want? I dont want any, I answered meekly. He could see I was weakening. Well, I'll throw in the records. Now If you'll sign your name on this line I'll have it sent around tomorrow. You can make the down payment now. Good old Brown, the Salesman's friend![50]

During production, a group of orphan children from Canada visited the Warner Brothers studios for a tour and got to watch Joe E. Brown film a scene for *Earthworm Tractors*:

> Popularity of Joe E. Brown among the kiddies was evidenced yesterday. He entertained forty children from the Church of Christ Children's home at Ontario on a tour of the Warner lot. The children, ranging from 2 to 16 years of age. watched the comedian make a sequence for his new picture, *Earthworm Tractors* and then they were taken around on other sets. By a popular vote taken in Ontario before making the trip to Hollywood, the youngsters, most of whom are orphans, chose Brown as their most popular

---

50 Joe E. Brown's Latest Picture. Mendocino Coast Beacon. October 3, 1936

movie star. The comedian promised to make a personal visit to their home sometime in the near future.[51]

It was a promise that Joe E. Brown later kept.

Earthworm Tractors is probably Joe E. Brown's most destructive comedy. The film's major highlights are when Botts is behind the wheel of a tractor and engaged in destruction. While these are very funny scenes, they are what originally soured Joe E. Brown on the project and caused him to avoid making it. Brown felt the comedy in the movie was too mechanical, and didn't stem from the actors. To an extent that is correct. However, some of the shots during these destructive slapstick sequences, such as a long shot of the tractor maneuvering over a rickety bridge, offered some remarkably good filmmaking.

Joe E. Brown still had many set-pieces in *Earthworm Tractors* that helped define his character. Perhaps the best of these is when Botts returns to the city after his trip back home reveals that Sally has married Emmett. He is told that Mabel went to Chicago to stay with her uncle, so Botts goes to Chicago, checks into a room, and calls every Johnson in the phone book, losing his voice in the process. When his vocal cords are pretty much shot, he leaves the phone booth and discovers that Mabel is the hotel operator. He was in the phone booth so long, that the operator who had been there when he arrived had finished her shift.

There are aspects of the Botts determination that work well within the parameters of Joe E. Brown's screen persona. But along with being a go-getter, Brown plays up the character's confidence, the lofty belief that he can do anything at optimal level. Unlike Elmer or Ike, for instance, Botts does not have the talent to back up his claims. What is fascinating about the way Joe E. Brown plays the role, is that while he often messes up, gets fired, et al, he never loses confidence, nor is there any indication that his confidence is a ploy. Botts truly, genuinely believes in himself, and when his botching the situation ends up achieving success in spite of itself, he gives himself the credit. Such a character could be insufferable, but, as with his boastful roles, Joe E. Brown makes Botts amusing and likable.

---

51 Around and About in Hollywood. *Los Angeles Times*. April 15, 1936

A good example of this is the montage that occurs when Botts first meets Johnson and tries to sell him the tractors—we see Botts repeatedly being thrown out, Johnson repeatedly telling him to go away (it escalates to the point where he throws Botts right through the door, Botts landing on a mattress, which is a funny visual). Botts does appear briefly discouraged when talking it over with Mabel afterward, but when she implies that a master salesman could show her dad how useful tractors can be, he immediately bounces back.

Earthworm Tractors further benefits from a strong supporting cast that includes the aforementioned Dick Foran and Guy Kibbee, as well as Gene Lockhart as a hotshot rival salesman. Each of these were firmly established and effective character performers. Foran had scored earlier in the year as the frustrated jock in *The Petrified Forest*, holding his own in a cast that included Humphrey Bogart in a breakout role, along with Bette Davis and Leslie Howard. Guy Kibbee was an old hand who had made gruffness an art unto itself, while the versatile Gene Lockhart excelled as kindly supportive characters and purely evil ones.

The women in more prominent roles, including June Travis and Carol Hughes, were comparative newcomers, but both were attractive and skilled at conveying the right emotion in either the comic or more serious scenes. Both women had just completed work on *Ceiling Zero* with James Cagney. Hughes also appeared the popular Al Jolson musical *The Singing Kid*. Hughes had a bit part in Brown's earlier movie *Bright Lights*.

Critics were pretty unanimous in their praise of this Joe E. Brown feature, realizing it didn't have the same grownup appeal as *Circus Clown, Bright Lights,* or *Sons O' Guns*, but Brown was in his element, true to form, and there was more than one report of kids laughing uproariously at the screenings. The critic for *Motion Picture Herald* stated:

> Anyone who likes comedy, hilarious amusement that leans heavily to the farcical, should get all he wants in this. The picture is all fun – even when it undertakes a romantic twist, the results are comic. Dialog, gags, characterizations, action, and situations are of a comedy pattern.[52]

---
52 Showman's Reviews. *Motion Picture Herald*. June 20, 1936

Joe poses on a massive tractor as a promotional shot for Earthworm Tractors

While elsewhere in other issues of the same trade periodical, exhibitors reported how well *Earthworm Tractors* went over with their audiences:

> Joe E. Brown pictures go over very well and one should not miss playing this picture.
>
> Can't be beat. Damn near busted the doors and did extra business.
>
> Another good peppy feature with Joe E. Brown. Joe always pleases.[53]

More than one reviewer noticed that, for perhaps the first time since he achieved any manner of stardom, Joe E. Brown does not once emit his famous yell in *Earthworm Tractors*. Even in the wild, destructive tractor sequences, the Brown yell is not added to the soundtrack in post-production.

There was a lot of irony connected to Brown during this period. Not only did he have to finally accept a film that he really didn't care to do, it turned out to be another very big hit. In fact, *Earthworm Tractors* was such a smash, it is one of the prime reasons that Joe reached his highest point among the top box office draws in 1936 at number 5. Thus, despite having signed up with an independent producer, the final movies Brown was making during his lame duck year with the studio, continued to be among his most popular.

But after completing *Earthworm Tractors*, Joe E. Brown had finally arrived upon the last project in his Warner Brothers contract. It seems fitting that the decision was made for Brown to end his long-time contract with this studio by appearing in another sports comedy.

---

53 What The Picture Did For Me. *Motion Picture Herald.* January 9, 1937

POLO JOE

Directed by William McGann
Screenplay: Peter Milne and Hugh Cummings
Produced by Bryan Foy
Cinematography: L. Wm. O'Connell
Film Editing: Clarence Kolster

Cast:

Joe E. Brown, Carol Hughes, Skeets Gallagher, Joe king, Gordon Elliot, Fay Holden, George E. Stone, Olive Tell, David Newell, Milton Kibbee, Frank Orth, John Kelly, Charley Foy, John Alexander, Louise Bates, Bess Flowers, Dick French, Edmund Mortmer, Elsa Peterson, William Worthington, Jane Wyman, Marc Cramer, Thomas Curran, Muriel Kearny, Shirley Lloyd, Wayne Morris, Anne Nagel, Jacqueline Saunders, Cyril Ring, Myrtle Steaman, Sam Rice, Ted Thompson, David Worth, Marjorie Weaver, Victoria Vinton, Bruce Warren, Perc Teeple, Ted Thompson, James Burtis, Harry Hollingsworth, Eddy Chandler, Max Hoffman Jr, Frank Darien, Sam McDaniel, Dudley Dickerson, Stuart Holmes, Leo McCabe, Bruce Warren, Guy Kingsford, Dong Yuen Jung.

Released December 8, 1936
Running time: 65 minutes
Warner Brothers
Black and White

While Joe E. Brown did make *Earthworm Tractors*, other projects such as *Cops and Robbers* announced some time ago, and an untitled Foreign Legion comedy, never did get produced. It was decided that Joe should close out his Warner Brothers contract with another sports comedy containing the formula that had worked so well for him in the past.

Richard "Skeets" Gallagher is Joe's valet in Polo Joe, *his last for Warner Brothers*

In *Polo Joe*, Joe plays an entitled rich boy with his own valet, Haywood (Skeets Gallgher). Joe returns home after spending time in China, and initially goes back to living with his Aunt Minnie (Fay Holden). Joe meets a pretty girl named Mary (Carol Hughes), but there is another man vying for Mary's interest. Don (Gordon Elliot) is a champion polo player. In order to attract Mary, Joe brags about being an even higher ranked polo player than Don, when in fact he has no experience, and his highly allergic to horses. His ruse seems to work when a set of circumstances result in his capturing a runaway horse and leading him back to its stall. Thus, Joe is entered in an important polo match and must find a way to get out of it and also save face. Joe and Haywood come up with a plan to pretend Joe has been kidnapped. However, Joe actually does get kidnapped and held for ransom by crooks who believe he really is a top polo star. Joe believes the actual kidnappers are the ones who were hired to do so. Once the crooks receive their ransom, they want to let Joe go. However, Joe needs to be in their custody until the polo match has ended so he fights them to remain in custody. Meanwhile, Don overheard Haywood and Joe planning the phony kidnapping and tries to prove it is all a ruse. And Haywood, realizing that Joe has been genuinely get kidnapped by actual crooks, leads the cops to the hideout and rescues him. Because of the timing of the situation, Joe must go ahead and play in the polo championship.

Very typical of Joe E. Brown's most noted comic formula, *Polo Joe* is not at the level of his baseball trilogy but remains a sincere and enjoyable movie to wrap up his highly successful film series at Warner Brothers. There are several comic highlights. The first happens very early in the film, when Joe is on a train that stops near a group of horses. His allergies kick in and he starts sneezing madly. Haywood attempts to shut the window, can't, and calls for the porter to help. Then the conductor comes in. Then some passengers come in to help. Pretty soon the train car is crowded with people attempting to close the window. This scene might have been inspired by the noted "stateroom sequence" in The Marx Brothers' MGM feature *A Night at the Opera*, released the year before.

Another highlight has Haywood bringing a donkey up to Joe's room at his Aunt's place so he can practice polo. Of course, the animal doesn't care to cooperate, causing destruction. Another is when the wild stallion Whirlwind escapes from its stall and gallops away, with Mary, Don, and Joe following by car, with Joe on the running board. The car goes over a bump, Joe flies in the air, and ends up on the horse's back. The animal gallops wildly, finally returning to his stall. When Don and Mary arrive soon afterward, it appears as though Joe handled the horse and brought it home.

Perhaps the funniest scene is when Joe is being held hostage by the crooks, and after receiving the ransom, they try to turn him loose. Rather than fighting to get away, Joe fights to remain in custody, and the battle offers some fun slapstick visuals. Joe subdues both men because they are so clumsy, they end up punching each other as Joe stands between them and ducks out of the way of their fists. Joe then swings from a chandelier on the ceiling and smacks each crook with a bottle. When Haywood bursts in with the police, Joe has both men tied up and has retrieved the ransom money.

Real life polo players Carl Crawford and Morgan Flowers joined Gordon Elliot and Joe to add authenticity to Polo Joe.

Polo Joe benefits from a good supporting cast, including Skeets Gallagher and Carol Hughes, both of whom Joe worked with on other movie projects. Fay Holden as his giggly aunt is a delight, a couple of years before settling into the role of Ma Hardy in the Andy Hardy series at MGM with Mickey Rooney. Gordon Elliot would later become known as Wild Bill Elliot and star in a series of popular western movies that ultimately defined his career.

During the filming of *Polo Joe*, a young visitor to the studio from England got a special thrill when brought to this set to watch Joe work. According to a press account:

> Joe E Brown and "Skeets" Gallagher were enacting comedy on the *Polo Joe* set when Joe spoiled one scene by waving a greeting. At the end of the scene Brown stopped to greet a gangling kid visitor. The boy's eyes popped out as Joe offered his hand and said "I'm Joe E. Brown. What's

your name?" The kid stammered that he was Robert Greenwood visiting from England. "Nice of you to come to see me," said Brown. "When I come to England, I'll visit you too." A trivial incident which you may regard lightly, but that moment will probably remain the highlight of the youngster's Hollywood visit.[54]

Critics were also pleased with this Joe E. Brown effort, with the review in the *San Francisco Examiner* stating: "It is probably Joe E. Brown's funniest picture. It is certainly one that he literally got many kicks out of during its filming. The story is unimportant. To ride a polo pony, or not to ride is the question Joe E. Brown had them squealing with glee at the matinee yesterday."[55]

There were some articles that were already anticipating what Joe was about to do next. Louella Parsons, for instance, anticipated that Joe was planning to do "a racetrack comedy" as his first production for David Loew. Others were under the impression that Joe would be employed with RKO studios, when in fact it was Loew with whom Brown was under contract. RKO was just the temporary distributor for Loew the producer.

Joe E. Brown was at the absolute height of his career. He was the highest paid actor at a major motion picture studio. He was the fifth most popular star in American motion pictures, the highest level he had achieved in his career, and surpassing other current comedians like The Marx Brothers, W.C. Fields, and Laurel and Hardy by a wide margin. And, he was about to begin a working relationship with an independent producer for more money per movie and greater creative control. It truly seemed that Joe E. Brown had everything going for him, and was about to embark on an exciting new plateau in his movie career that promised a very positive progression that would benefit him at every level.

Many years later, when he wrote his autobiography *Laughter is a Wonderful Thing*, Joe E. Brown would look back on his decision to leave Warner Brothers and sign with David Loew as "a disastrous move."

---

54 Joe Spoils The Scene. *San Pedro News-Pilot.* July 23, 1936
55 Joe E Brown Scores Another Comedy Hit. *The San Francisco Chronicle.* November 28, 1936

WHEN'S YOUR BIRTHDAY

Directed by Harry Beaumont
Screenplay: Harry Clork from the play by Fred Ballard, adapted by Harvey Gates, Malcolm Stuart Boylan, and Samuel M. Pike.
Produced by David L Loew
Cinematography: George Robinson
Film Editing: Jack Ogilvie

Cast:
Joe E. Brown, Marian Marsh, Fred Keating, Edgar Kennedy, Maude Eburne, Suzanne Kaaren, Margaret Hamilton, Minor Watson, Frank Jenks, Don Rowan, Granville Bates, Charles Judels, Murray Alper, Don "Red" Barry, Ward Bond, Harrison Greene, Maria Shelton, Jack Perry, Lee Phelps, Ronald Rondell, Bull Montana, Jimmy O'Gatty, Ruth Robin, Dennis O'Keefe, Hal Price, Eddie Kane, Bert Moorehouse, Tom Kennedy, Ted Oliver, Maria Shelton, Thomas Jackson, Sam Hayes, Edward Earle, Billy Coe, Jay Eaton, Kit Guard, Jack Chefe, Bobby Barber, Manny Harmon and his Orchestra.

Released February 19, 1937
Running time: 75 minutes
David L. Loew productions for RKO Radio Pictures
Black and White

Before he embarked on his highly anticipated first movie with an independent producer, Joe E. Brown took his family on a trip to Europe. Upon his return, he was eager to embark on the next step in his movie career. At the time, it seemed like a great deal and was celebrated in the press.

An organization has been assembled by David L. Loew for his production of *When's Your Birthday*, the first Joe E.

Brown comedy to be released by RKO Radio studio. The Loew company will be a separate unit. Robert Harris will be associate producer, and Harry Beaumont director. Richard MacCaulay, H. W. Haneman and Harry Clark are writing the Brown feature. It's long been a legend of movieland that comedy stars do best when working independently, so the Loew set-up seems adroit. The picture is expected to start November 9.[56]

Not only was Joe E. Brown's first independent production in process, but Loew anticipated real success and bought more projects:

Nothing if not serene is the future of Joe E. Brown as a comedy star. Three picture subjects have already been selected for him by David L. Loew, who is producing the output independently for RKO release. *When's Your Birthday*, the first feature, will be followed by *Flirting With Fate*, and after that will come *All This Confusion*, written by Richard Macauley, who will also do the screenplay. Loew has assembled full personnel for his organization, including technicians, cameramen, other principal assistants, and is making the films at RKO.[57]

By all accounts, this looked like a real career advancement for Brown, with more money and greater creative input

It is unfortunate that *When's Your Birthday* is such a disappointment. Not that attempts weren't being made to come up with a good movie. The cast is filled with welcome veterans like Edgar Kennedy, Maude Eburne, Granville Bates, Margaret Hamilton, Minor Watson, and Frank Jenks. Marian Marsh is an attractive co-star, as is Suzanne Kaaren, best remembered as Dolores in the 3 Stooges classic *What's the Matador*. But a flat script and lackluster direction give these top talents very little to work with.

The premise has promise. Joe plays Dustin Willoughby, who is studying astrology in order to become a "D.A.: Director of Astrology." Dustin's firm belief that the alignment of the stars and planets

---

56 Brown Comedy Unit Assembles. *Los Angels Times*. November 3, 1936
57 Joe E. Brown Chooses Third Comedy Under New Production Setup. *Los Angeles Times*. November 4, 1936

Publicity portrait of Joe E. Brown for When's Your Birthday, *his first for independent producer David Loew*

dictate everything is borne out in a series of circumstances where his astrological-based predictions come true. It jeopardizes his personal life. His fiancee wants a June wedding, but Dustin insists July is the better month. And whether he is taking on amateur boxing matches or working as a nightclub waiter, Dustin's success or failure is based on what his horoscope indicates. On a night when the stars and planets do not line up cohesively in his zodiac sign's favor, he spends the evening being pummeled in the ring, or succumbing to destructive clumsiness in the nightclub. Some gamblers employ him for his ability to accurately predict race results, but when they try to engage in Dustin's methods, they mix up his astrological chart with that of a small time Salvadorian boxer. Thinking the boxer is perfectly set to win the championship, they fly him in for the bout. When they discover it was Dustin's chart they were looking at, they

David Loew productions promoted the fact that they had signed a major star like Joe E. Brown for a series of films.

force him into the ring. Fortunately, Dustin does have a boxing background and holds his own in the bout.

While the premise of *When's Your Birthday* is interesting it doesn't feel like it was pushed to its full potential. The majority of the film is just Dustin explaining astrological signs to disbelievers, which could easily result in better comedy than what we get here. This sort of premise might have worked a bit better at Warner Brothers, where writers and directors familiar with Joe E. Brown could have constructed the film more solidly. Screenwriter Harry Clark was fairly new to writing for films and had no real experience writing comedy. Director Harry Beaumont had been successful in the 20s and helmed the Oscar winner *Broadway Melody* (1929), but he was also a novice when it came to this type of comedy. Production values are noticeably lower, and while Joe works hard, there really isn't much for him to work with.

With every Joe E. Brown film thus far, there are particular highlights that can be pointed out. However, the only comic highlights here are blackout gags, such as a potted plant falling on a judge's head after Dustin warns him that his horoscope is so bad, he should have stayed home that day. The boxing match was choreographed nicely as well, as this film, like its predecessors showcases Brown's athletic ability.

Ironically, the best scene in *When's Your Birthday* doesn't feature Joe E. Brown at all. It is an animated dream sequence that opens the film. Originally shot in Technicolor (a color print does not appear to have survived), the sequence is historically important for being the first animation directed or supervised by Robert Clampett. Cartoon producer Leon Schlesinger was hired by David Loew to produce the animated sequence, which is astrologically based and presented as a dream Dustin has after being knocked out in a boxing match.

At the time, Bob Clampett was animating for Schlesinger's studio in and badly wanted to direct. Schlesinger gave Clampett this sequence to test his abilities, and the opening sequence, only minutes long, is more amusing than the rest of the movie. The importance of this sequence being Robert Clampett's first directed animation is, perhaps, more noteworthy than the feature being Joe E. Brown's first independent production. Clampett went on to direct such animated classics as *Porky in Wackyland* and *Corny Concerto*. In television, he created the *Beany and Cecil* show. The fact that the film has such a creative opening suggests that the rest of the film will be just as clever, so it's even more of a disappointment that it isn't.

It has been claimed in other studies that *When's Your Birthday* did not do well at the box office because it being a low-budget independent production resulted in its being played in fewer theaters, overall, than a movie from a major studio like Warner Brothers. Actually, since David Loew had struck a deal with RKO as his distributor, it played in as many theaters and was not limited to smaller neighborhood houses. It should be remembered that in 1937 Joe E. Brown was one of the five most popular stars in movies, and coming off his most successful years in films. RKO had already produced the very popular *King Kong* and was currently producing

Joe boxes Jimmy O'Gatty in When's Your Birthday

the Fred Astaire-Ginger Rogers musicals. So, the distribution, and interest from exhibitors, was definitely at the A-picture level for this B-picture. The reaction from moviegoers, however, was disappointment:

> A very poor Brown picture.
>
> The general opinion seemed to be that it was not as good as preceding Joe E. Brown pictures.
>
> The picture isn't funny it's silly.
>
> Poorly produced.
>
> Joe E. Brown has about lost out. He used to be one of our best liked players.[58]

Brown wasn't completely written off after one weak movie, of course, but this indicates what a comedown *When's Your Birthday* had been, despite the enthusiasm of Joe embarking on a new series of independently produced features.

While Joe E. Brown had faltered once before, with the offbeat *A Very Honorable Guy* that disappointed his moviegoing fans, he quickly bounced back with his next movie. And he did it this time as well, but not nearly as decidedly. Because, while *Riding on Air* is a better movie than *When's Your Birthday*, it has its own set of problems.

---

58 What the Picture Did For Me. *The Motion Picture Herald.* Various 1937 issues.

RIDING ON AIR

Directed by Edward Sedgwick
Screenplay: Richard Macaulay and Richard Flournoy based on a character created by Macaulay
Produced by David L Loew
Cinematography: Alfred Gilks
Film Editing: Jack Ogilvie

Cast:
Joe E. Brown, Guy Kibbee, Florence Rice, Vinton Hayworth, Anthony Nace, Harlan Briggs, Frank Sully, Andrew Tombes, Clem Bevans, Harry C. Bradley, Robert Emmett O'Connor, George Lloyd, Tom Dugan, Don Brodie, Monte Collins, George Chandler, Jack Norton, Joseph Creehan, Lester Dorr, Kernan Cripps, Charlie Hall, Murray Alper, Henry Roquemore, Dennis O'Keefe, Si Jenks, Budd Buster, Benny Burt.

Released June 18, 1937
Running time: 70 minutes
David L. Loew productions for RKO Radio Pictures
Black and White
Alternate title: *All is Confusion*

Joe E. Brown's later belief that his leaving Warner Brothers for indie features with David Loew was a disaster is because he went from one of the nation's top box office stars to a B-level movie comedian. While there is a great deal of respect for B movies from film historians in the 21st century, back when these films were made, these lower budget productions were dismissed as secondary. However, Joe was still popular despite the fact that his anticipated first indie movie was a disappointment. And *Riding on Air* is, at least, a marginal improvement.

Trade ad for Riding On Air

The movie was based on a *Saturday Evening Post* character created by Richard Macauley, who also penned the screenplay. This recalled other successful Brown comedies using characters from *Saturday Evening Post* stories like *Alibi Ike* and *Earthworm Tractors*.

At the time of the film's release, moviegoers would be familiar with the magazine stories, and would connect this character with Joe E. Brown.

However, while it was taken from the actual stories themselves, it was decided that the original title, *All is Confusion* was unsatisfactory:

> To Mr. and Mrs. Movie Public, titling a film production would appear to be a minor detail. But take it from David L. Loew, producer of the Joe E. Brown starring pictures, selection of a good release title can frequently be a headache looming ultimately to the proportions of a major catastrophe. Until he finally chose *Riding On Air* for the title of Brown's current feature, recently previewed and shortly to be released for the general public, screen titles had been chasing the producer in his dreams. When they began shooting the picture, based upon the series of Elmer Lane stories written by Richard Macaulay for the Saturday Evening Post, they used *All Is Confusion* for the working title. This was the name of one of the magazine stories, but considered weak for the screen, When Shakespeare uttered his now trite but nevertheless classic query, "What's in a name?" he couldn't have anticipated the advent of movies. At any rate, Loew gave impetus to the search for a release title for Brown's latest effort by offering a reward. Many were submitted but few found favor with the powers that be. Among the few was *Riding On Air*, which the producer liked but wanted to save for another picture. Director Edward Sedgwick came forward with *Sky High*, the title of a Tom Mix opus he had once directed in the silent era for Fox studios, and which Loew instantly liked. Twentieth Century-Fox was contacted and bestowed its blessing upon, the Loew company's borrowing it. Loew thought his troubles were over. But. alas, not for long. The Tom Mix picture had been made so long ago that Fox's right to the title had since expired, and it was subsequently re-registered by two other film companies. Then confusion literally threatened to engulf the company, but the producer avoided further difficulties by deciding to use *Riding On Air* for the release title.

Joe and Florence Rice in Riding on Air

Elmer Lane is a Claremont Wisconsin newspaperman whose life is filled with hobbies from gadgetry, to HAM radio, to piloting his own plane. It is, at first, a good character for Joe E. Brown, allowing him to exhibit his established screen persona's enthusiasm for different things. Elmer is particularly interested in his aviator friend Bill's (Anthony Nace) radio beam invention. He also longs to buy the paper he works for. After winning $5000 in an essay contest, Elmer prepares to buy the newspaper, but is talked into investing into a company featuring Bill's invention by con man Doc Waddington (Guy Kibbee). Elmer's girl Betty (Florence Rice) is so chagrined by this decision, she starts to see Elmer's hotshot newspaper rival Harvey Schumann (Vinton Hayworth). Harvey discovers a gangster's dead body in a field, and tricks Elmer into delivering the photographs to a rival paper. Elmer gets involved with perfume smugglers who are responsible for the gangster's death, and a wild climax has him chasing them in Bill's plane.

Despite it being a bit of an improvement over *When's Your Birthday*, and being better received by period moviegoers, *Riding on Air*

Joe longs to be a newspaper reporter in Riding on Air

is still a disappointment. Much of this has to do with Joe's character. In his Warner movies, whether he was playing a shy milquetoast or a swaggering braggart, Joe's characters were always particularly skillful or smart. In *Riding On Air*, Joe plays Elmer as an amiable bumbler who is foolish and easily duped. In fact, at one point, his girlfriend Betty says of his planning to enter the essay contest, "the only contest you could win is for being the dumbest man in the world!" This isn't during an argument, or when the girl is mad, nor is it delivered as caustic or wisecracking. She says this with affection borne from pity because Elmer simply isn't particularly good at anything. When Elmer does win the contest, Betty is upset by his choice to invest. In each case, Elmer is presented as an earnest dumbbell. When he figures out the complexity of the gangster's murder, his explanation to patrons at a barber shop is laughed at. When he leaves, he breaks the glass on the door as he slams it. Even the moment where Elmer shows some pragmatism, the scene is punctuated with comedy to make him look silly.

Joe parachutes to a successful landing in Riding on Air

Riding on Air attempts to present a folksy charm in the tradition of the original *Saturday Evening Post* short stories, and Joe E. Brown always registers well as a small town citizen. But, unlike his earlier movies, the small town doesn't respect him as one in whom they can have some pride due to his accomplishments or skills. He's just another dope who is responsible for one gaffe after another.

The climactic airplane chase is the film's highlight, and Edward Sedgwick is a good director for this type of material, but the budgetary restrictions force the scene to be cheaply presented with a reliance on phony back projection effects. Even a final fall with a parachute that opens at the last minute looks too cheap to be very exciting.

Still, the film was far better received than *When's Your Birthday* when it was released to theaters, and Joe E. Brown's name still managed top-of-the-bill bookings in double-feature programs. Exhibitors reported that it played to capacity business. Even when it was screened at a State Prison in Trenton, New Jersey, the result was positive:

Joe and Florence Rice are up a tree in Riding on Air

Here is one of those light, nonsensical comedies that will keep your customers bouncing around in their seats. The men here thoroughly enjoyed it and their gusts of laughter were a tonic to hear. There isn't much to the plot, but Joe E. Brown carries it along and establishes himself as one of the best comedians on the screen.

Meanwhile, critics were also kinder to this Joe E. Brown offering, with one review stating:

Although the middle initial of Joe E. Brown doesn't stand for Entertainment, his newest picture, *Riding on Air*, certainly does. For the film is crammed with inspired comedy, thrills that have audiences holding onto their seats, and the best Joe E. Brown pantomime. The latter is something generally unexcelled by any comedian today on our screen.[59]

---

59 Joe E. Brown on Twin Bill. *Santa Cruz Evening News*. July 1, 1937

Riding on Air also features the gratification of Elmer coming out on top at the end of the movie, proving he was right, winning the girl, getting a big welcome home from the town, and making Bill's invention a million-dollar success. But it still pales in comparison to the movies he did at Warner Brothers.

According to an article in *Film Daily*, Joe E. Brown had a rather interesting gig immediately after completing production on *Riding on Air*:

> The head of the Child Welfare League of America expressed a desire to have Joe E. Brown officiate at their annual May Day celebration. Joe hurried completion of his picture *Riding on Air* and made a special trip to New York at his own expense. Joe loves kids, the tougher the better, and he got 'em plenty tough when he umpired a baseball game in the tenement district on the east side. Joe made a close decision and almost started a riot.[60]

Joe moved quickly into filming his next David Loew production, *Fit for a King*, which would be his last under the RKO distribution deal. Loew was also reported as looking for another star to produce:

> David Loew, head man of the Joe E. Brown pictures, is one producer who is not looking for new screen faces. Just give him one more established personality on a box-office par with Joe, and he will be happy. To prove he means what he says, he's going on a "big name" hunt in New York and Europe, hoping to find another star whose box office draw is sufficient to warrant production expansion of Loew pictures beyond the current three-a-year starring Joe. The present Brown opera, *Fit For a King*, will wind up the RKO release agreement. Then Joe and the "new star" (if found) will move to Columbia.[61]

No new star was found, but Loew continued to produce Joe E. Brown features, as the comedian had four more on his contract.

---

60 Great Guy Joe E. Brown. *Film Daily*. May 7, 1937
61 Producer Looking for Old Talent. *San Francisco Examiner*. June 18, 1937

FIT FOR A KING

Directed by Edward Sedgwick
Screenplay: Richard Flournoy
Produced by David L Loew
Cinematography: Paul Vogel
Film Editing: Jack Ogilvie

Cast:
Joe E. Brown, Helen Mack, Paul Kelly, Harry Davenport, Halliwell Hobbes, John Qualen, Donald Briggs, Robert Warwick, Frank Reicher, Russell Hicks, Charles Trowbridge, Dorothy Appleby, George Renavent, Zeffie Tibury, Charles Lane, Johnny Arthur, James Flavin, Pat O'Malley, Josef Swickard, Edward Keane, John Graham Spacey, Ann Codee, William O'Brien, P.J. Kelly, Jack Rutherford, Barbara Barondess, Elsa Janssen, Eugene Borden, Jean DeBriac, Doris Rankin, Shirley Chambers, Harry Cording.

Released September 1, 1937
Running time: 73 minutes
David L. Loew productions for RKO Radio Pictures
Black and White

Just as *Riding on Air* had been an improvement over *When's Your Birthday*, so then is *Fit for a King* better than *Riding on Air*. But none of these are as good as Joe E. Brown's Warner Brothers efforts.

This one features Joe E. Brown as Scoops Jackson, a reporter on the Daily Blade only because his uncle owns the paper. Scoops is another earnest bumbler, but despite limited skills, he longs to get an assignment to cover a major story. At present he is merely an errand boy. A blurb comes over the wire about a long-exiled Archduke trapped in an elevator that plummets several stories until the emergency break saves him. The managing editor of the blade thinks so little of it, he sends Scoops to cover it. He then discov-

Trade ad for Fit for a King

ers the rival newspaper sent their best man, Briggs, because the story is much bigger than he had realized. This allows Scoops to prove himself. Scoops and Briggs are rivals for the same story so each tries to thwart the other while attempting to gather their own information. While Scoops is in disguise, he meets Jane Hamilton from Kansas and falls for her, not realizing she is actually a Princess. It is discovered that the Archduke, exiled since 1918, is visiting his sister at a sanitarium in Vichy, France, so both Scoops and Briggs head there. Scoops ends up thwarting a plan to stage the death of the Princess at the hands of the military, while Jane decides she doesn't want to be a Princess, she wants to marry Scoops.

When we are first introduced to Scoops, he is bringing the managing editor (Russell Hicks) his sandwich. Barely given the least amount of attention, when Scoops quietly inquires about the possibility of more work as a reporter, the editor reacts angrily, accusing him as using his uncle's influence to curry favor. In fact, Scoops comes off as earnest, willing to try his best – but is also presented as yet another bumbler who doesn't deserve much more than delivery errands. Scoops gets the same negative reaction from reporter (Charles Lane) who simply doesn't want him in the way.

Joe E. Brown is once again playing a sympathetic character who connects with the audience with his genuineness, his willingness to try and to work hard. The immediate and caustic reactions to him further establish him as a put-upon innocent. This character structure is as old as comedy itself, and it seems like a good direction for Joe, based on his unimpressive debut films after signing with David Loew.

One of the film's first highlights occurs when Scoops is on board a ship chasing the story. Briggs (Paul Kelly), the man from the rival newspaper, plays a trick on Scoops which gets him in trouble and thrown in the brig. The highlight is when Scoops tries to maintain some sort of balance as the ship rocks over the bumpy waves in the ocean. Director Edward Sedgwick, whose career dated back to silent comedy, was a master at this sort of visual gag. He holds a medium shot on Scoops, behind bars, sitting at a table that slides back and forth as the boat rocks. Scoops is stumbling around, trying to keep balance, knocking open porthole doors and allowing water to come splashing in. The bit lasts several minutes, is without dialog, and is one of the funnier scenes that Joe E. Brown has performed.

However, the biggest highlight is the slapstick climax where Scoops hurries to his destination on a motorcycle's sidecar, with a hay wagon, a train car, and, finally, a bicycle. Sedgwick really offers some very creative visual images during these fast-paced moments. Scoops has disguised himself as an enemy soldier as he rides in a sidecar of a motorcycle driven by another solider. When his helmet is knocked off, Scoops sticks his head in his jacket to conceal his identity. The driver looks, sees a headless man, and jumps off the vehicle. Scoops crashes and steals a wagon filled with hay. The wagon gradually falls apart as it sails down the paths, while hoboes who are hiding in the hay come tumbling out. When the only thing left is the front of the wagon where Scoops sits and the horses, it gives the illusion of a chariot. After exhaustingly pumping a train car, Scoops finally ends up on a bicycle, bumping along as he rides it across railroad tracks. Period distributors recalled that these scenes resulted in gales of laughter from their moviegoers.

Joe and Helen Mack in Fit for a King

Critics responded favorably to *Fit for a King*, as did audiences. It was Joe E. Brown's biggest box office success since *Polo Joe*, and David Loew was pleased at the momentum Brown was generating with each successive vehicle. But, Joe had plummeted from the Top 5 box office stars to the bottom rung of the Top 20 – not a bad place to be, but quite a comedown from where he once was. *Fit For a King* was usually the bottom half of a double bill at the major theaters, as Joe was now considered a B movie actor. But, it was heartening to read such reactions as this one from a theater owner in Indiana:

> As good a comedy as Joe E. Brown ever made. This one is a knockout. Brown is one actor who shows he can put it across, no matter who his producer or director is. Joe's Bicycle ride and hayrack stunt is tops.

Apparently, the David Loew production unit was starting to understand what to do with Joe E. Brown – how to use his talents most effectively. Although he was now in his mid-forties, he still had the athletic prowess to perform slapstick effectively. And director Edward Sedgwick was very good at staging slapstick sequences. The low budgets were a problem, but a bit of ingenuity resulted in a rather well staged end sequence with the hay truck, bicycle, etc.

And the modification of Joe E. Brown's character continued to be explored. In *Fit for a King* he is another bumbler whose success is more stumbled into than achieved from his own skills, but Scoops is presented as determined and confident, which are character traits that had worked in his earlier films, so that his triumph in the end seems more determined.

Some curious period criticisms pointed out that Brown was playing too much of a ladies' man in these films. That's odd, because in all of his Warner movies, he wins over the pretty girl despite not having classic good looks. In these films there are elements of his character that attract pretty women in basically the same manner. He is never purported to be traditionally handsome.

Fit for a King was Joe E. Brown's final David Loew production to be released by RKO. The studio was no longer interested in the product after the contract ended, so Loew went looking for another distributor. He found one in Columbia Pictures. Although he was considered a very difficult, challenging person to deal with, Columbia studio head Harry Cohn did appreciate comedians. In 1934 he hired Jules White away from MGM to start a comedy short subject unit at the studio, resulting in the timelessly popular Three Stooges series, as well as second chance gigs for silent movie comedians like Buster Keaton, Harry Langdon, Charley Chase, and Andy Clyde. Thus, Cohn felt that Joe E. Brown would be a good performer for the studio to distribute, if not produce themselves.

Fit for a King was promising as being his best film since leaving Warner Brothers, and it appeared there would be a positive change in his indie movies as a result. For his first film to be released through Columbia, Joe E. Brown's screen character seemed to be a return to form.

WIDE OPEN FACES

Directed by Kurt Neuman
Screenplay: Earle Snell, Clarence Marks, Joe Bigelow, Pat C. Flick from a story by Richard Flournoy
Produced by David L Loew
Cinematography: Paul Vogel
Film Editing: Jack Ogilvie

Cast:
Joe E. Brown, Jane Wyman, Alison Skipworth, Lyda Roberti, Alan Baxter, Lucien Littlefiled, Sidney Toler, Berton Churchill, Barbara Pepper, Joe Downing, Stanley Fields, Garry Owen, Dick Rich, Walter Willis, Duke York, Robert McKenzie, Joe Marks, Horace Murphy, Dudley Dickerson, Junior Hughes, Elwyn Hoffman, Jack Perry, Charles Sullivan, Al Hill, Lester Dorr, Bert Moorhouse, Dorothy Vernon, Sam Hayes.

Released April 18, 1938
Running time: 67 minutes
David L. Loew productions for Columbia Pictures
Black and White

After David Loew secured a two-movie distribution deal with Columbia Pictures, there was some talk of a project that would team Joe with that studio's successful comedy team The Three Stooges. The Stooges had been the stars of Jules White's short comedy productions at Columbia since signing there four years earlier, but had made only sporadic cameo appearances in feature films. One of the ideas that generated some press was a film called *Chinese Hooey*:

> Joe E Brown's first starring vehicle to be released by Columbia will be *Chinese Hooey*, in which the current Sino-Japanese war will be the background. Featured with

Brown in the David L. Loew production will be Howard, Fine, and Howard, Columbia's Three Stooges short subject stars in their first feature appearance. Edward Sedgwick will direct.[62]

This idea apparently fell through, but when it was settled that *Wide Open Faces* would be the first Joe E. Brown production for Columbia, the Stooges were also initially attached to that movie according to the trades. However, by the time shooting was underway in December of 1937, the Stooges were no longer part of the production.

Lyda Roberti and Joe in Wide Open Faces

---

62 Set New Brown Film. *Motion Picture Daily.* October 17, 1937

Joe E. Brown stars as Wilbur Meeks, a soda jerk who is with Duke Temple (Stanley Fields), a notorious gangster, when he is finally captured by the FBI. This gangster is known for having stashed a large bankroll and several different gangs believe Wilbur may have an idea as to its whereabouts. So they all descend upon a rundown hotel that Wilbur is helping to get reactivated because he is smitten with Betty (Jane Wyman), a girl who has inherited the inn with her Aunt Martha (Alison Skipworth). The gangsters check in, believing Duke's loot is stashed somewhere, and proceed to wreck the hotel looking for it. Gangster Tony's moll Kitty (Lyda Roberti) tries to romance it out of Wilbur, much to Betty's chagrin. Finally, the crooks discover the money, tie Wilbur up and escape. Wilbur is released by Betty and the two pursue the gangsters with the sheriff (Sidney Toler) pursuing them.

Wide Open Faces starts out very promisingly, presenting Joe E. Brown's Wilbur Meeks character as confident and skilled in the old Warner Brothers tradition. Wilbur works at a soda fountain owned by Pop (Lucien Littlefield) that has a jump in customers when a bus pulls up at a certain time each day. He has a photographic memory and deft hands when it comes to remembering and filling orders, so we see him tossing donuts to a patron holding up his fork, rapidly mixing fountain drinks and sliding them to the proper customer, and even flicking a cherry on a sundae from afar. It is all very amusing and nicely shot. The only problem is, the entire premise is jettisoned after this scene. As the film goes on, Wilbur never utilizes these skills as a part of his character.

Wilbur's display of confidence, at least initially, seems to be a major part of his character. He struts behind the counter of the soda fountain and effortlessly takes care of the crowd rush to everyone's satisfaction. And he maintains this aspect of the character when he meets Betty and her Aunt, has to confront crooks, needs to stand up to the sheriff, and ultimately pursues and captures the gangsters who take the money. Even as he is being tied up, he isn't the quivering bumbler of earlier Loew films, he bravely and confidently stands up to the gangsters, threatening to get even if he has to follow them to the ends of the earth. It is a welcome throwback to the characters of the earlier films, and distracts us from the fact

Jane Wyman, Alison Skipworth, and Joe in Wide Open Faces

that *Wide Open Faces* just isn't a very good movie. Along with an inconsistent set of character traits for Wilbur, the tone of the movie is inconsistent. For instance, there is an attempt at some spooky vibes when Wilbur first goes to the abandoned inn. This isn't that type of movie so this sequence seems out of place in context.

Perhaps the main highlight of the film is a dance bit Wilbur performs with Betty, as it features Joe E. Brown dancing in a movie for the first time since leaving Warners. The climactic chase is a lot of wacky fun, even allowing one to overlook the rear projection and obvious stock footage. Betty and Wilbur are bickering at the outset, but a box of tear gas bombs starts smoking in the back seat causing both to cry uncontrollably during their argument, and, thus, each feels sorry for the other. Betty takes the wheel and Joe tosses the active tear gas into the various cars chasing them, leaving only the car that the sheriff is manning along with Aunt Martha (Joe having taken the sheriff's own car).

It is fun to see Jane Wyman in an early role. She has good chemistry with Brown, especially in the scenes where their relationship was a little more contentious. It is also fun to see Sidney Toler just before he'd be defining his career by taking over the Charlie Chan role upon the death of actor Warner Oland. Lucien Littlefield is a veteran character actor whose career includes some memorable roles in the Laurel and Hardy comedies *Dirty Work* and *Sons of the Desert*. Alison Skipworth had scored in films with W.C. Fields and Mae West. And the various gangsters were played by such familiar faces as Joe Downing, Duke York, and Al Hill. Of course, Stanley Fields, who plays Red, was a notable presence in the gangster classic *Little Caesar*.

Lyda Roberti had made a big impact with W.C. Fields and Jack Oakie in *Million Dollar Legs* several years earlier, and had recently replaced the late Thelma Todd and teamed with Patsy Kelly for some comedies at the Hal Roach studio. Shortly after filming completed on *Wide Open Faces*, Lyda was diagnosed with a heart ailment and told to quit movies. She and her husband became very short on money, and started building up debts they could not cover. In January of 1938, grocer William F. Webb sued the couple for their not having paid for food he had delivered to their home. On March 12, 1938, Lyda was sitting on her bed, bending over to tie her shoe, when she suffered a fatal heart attack. Joe E. Brown was among many celebrities to send a floral tribute to her funeral.

By the time *Wide Open Faces* was released in April of 1938, Joe E. Brown's name had left the Top Box Office polls and he was considered a B movie actor whose films were primarily for kids. *Wide Open Faces* played the bottom half of double bills where it'd be paired in a major movie house with a big studio A-picture like *Jezebel* on the top tier, or would play neighborhood theaters with a B western headlining the program. Joe was still popular, but as B-movie journeyman, no longer as a major movie star. His movies were now comic quickies to warm up the audience for the main feature – they were no long the main feature themselves.

Even though he would later state how unhappy he was during this period of his career, Joe E. Brown never walked through a film with any indifference. He always gave 100%, even in a more lackluster movie, making it as good as he can. Sometimes the script just isn't easy for him to salvage with his antics.

However, Joe E. Brown's next film under the Columbia distribution deal returned him to sports comedy and *The Gladiator* turned out to be one of the very best movies of his entire career.

THE GLADIATOR

Directed by Edward Sedgwick
Screenplay: Charles Melson and Arthur Sheekman from a story by Phillip Wylie adapted by James Mulhauser and Earle Snell
Produced by David L Loew
Cinematography: Paul Vogel
Film Editing: Jack Ogilvie

Cast:
Joe E. Brown, June Travis, Man Mountain Dean, Dickie Moore, Lucien Littlefield, Robert Kent, Ethel Wales, Donald Douglas, Eddie Kane, Lee Phelps, Wright Kramer, Pat McKee, Jack Perry, Dee Dodd, Robert Winkler, William Gould, Harrison Greene, Lloyd Ingraham, Marjorie Kane, Edward LeSaint, Charles Wilson, Milton Kibbee, Charles Sullivan, Frank Mills, John Shelton, Jack Mulhall, Harry Semels, Jack Perry, Lee Phelps, Richard Alexander, Dee Dodd.

Released August 15, 1938
Running time: 72 minutes
David L. Loew productions for Columbia Pictures
Black and White

The Gladiator is a veritable oasis in the desert, rising high above his other indie films for David Loew, and ranking alongside his very best work. It was a refreshing return to sports comedy and utilized the best qualities of Joe E. Brown's screen persona to make him seem charming and amiable rather than earnest and bumbling. His screen character was complex enough to be presented as a swaggering braggart for the first time since *Alibi Ike*.

There was a rumor connected to this simple comedy that it inspired Jerry Siegel and Joe Schuster to create the Superman comic. Well, that's not quite possible. Superman's origins date back to 1933, and

Ad for The Gladiator, *Brown's best movie for David Loew*

while it was sold to Detective Comics in 1938, the first comic book came out two months before this movie was released. The rumor then shifted to the possibility that the 1930 Phillip Wyllie novel on which this comedy is based, inspired Superman, but Mr. Siegel has said this is not so.

Despite it not having influenced Superman, this comedy featuring Joe E. Brown is delightfully super-heroic. Joe plays Hugo Kipp, a worker at an orphanage whom the kids love, especially little Bobby (Dickie Moore). Hugo is told that in order to remain in his current position, a new corporate rule indicates he must have a college degree. Hugo had attended college 12 years earlier as a Freshman so he enrolls as a sophomore at the same University where both his father and grandfather had been star athletes. Because of his lineage, Joe is talked into joining the football team, but his lack of skills makes him little more than a laughingstock. This changes when Hugo is used as a guinea pig by his landlord, Professor Danner (Lucien Littlefield); a wacky scientist who works at the college. Danner injects Hugo with a serum containing the qualities of an ant (allowing him to lift several times his own weight) and a grasshopper (allowing him to jump several times his own height). Joe's status on the football team changes, when in the next practice he mows down the others. Playing in the big game, Hugo succeeds in knocking over the competition and jumping over the approaching line. However, later on, when Hugo desperately tries to earn money by going two-out-of-three falls with massive professional wrestler Man Mountain Dean, the serum runs out in mid-match.

The Gladiator is charmingly funny without pretension, and remains consistently entertaining throughout its running time. Always relaxing and pleasant, *The Gladiator* is also filled with several big comedy scenes providing good laughs. A pre-serum Hugo is used as a tackling dummy, offering a running commentary ("this is the best sawdust I ever tasted!"). Unfortunately, Joe E. Brown tore a tendon in his right leg while filming this scene.

Hugo Kipp is a much more layered character than Brown had played in any of his other David Loew productions. He has a job, at which he is successful. He accepts the necessity of going to college to keep that job. He responds romantically to Iris Bennett, played

Joe becomes a star on the gridiron when he returns to college in The Gladiator

by June Travis who had worked with Brown at Warners in *Earthworm Tractors*. He responds negatively to being duped by the team, a throwback to a similar situation in *Elmer The Great*. And after he realizes his strength, he struts, swaggers and brags in the same manner as Elmer. The romance with Iris even has a complexity similar to the one with Patricia Ellis in *Elmer The Great*. Kipp chooses to avoid playing football when Professor Danner tells him he could seriously hurt or even kill someone. Iris is recruited to romance him into playing for the team. Kipp discovers he's been duped just as Elmer does in the earlier movie. And, also similarly, she genuinely falls for him after she has betrayed him. Robert Kent plays the typical jealous jock who feels overshadowed by Hugo's prowess.

Joe E. Brown's scenes with disabled orphan Dickie Moore are very moving, adding yet another layer to Hugo's character. The

Joe's handshake is too much for Man Mountain Dean, as Jack Perry and Pat McKee observe

scenes involving Dickie Moore and the orphanage could have easily come off as trite, but thanks to the performances the interactions between the characters feel genuine and they contribute to the story rather than hindering it.

It is this relationship that Iris uses to entice Hugo into playing for the team. She realizes that her feminine wiles pale in comparison to his feelings for the youngster. He decides to "be careful." The scene where Kip runs the field jumping over the oncoming players from the opposing team is quite funny, including the cutaways to spectators reacting. Ever the nice guy, Kip waits at the goal and hands the ball to a fellow player so he can make the touchdown.

The concluding wrestling bout is both funny and exciting. It is well choreographed as both men are using genuine pro wrestling moves. Man Mountain Dean was an actual wrestler who had given up the ring for a movie career, so he had an understanding as to how to work in the ring while still responding to the camera. Joe did his own stunts in the ring. However, at one point, when Hugo lifts massive Man Mountain Dean onto his shoulders for the airplane spin, it sent Joe E. Brown to the hospital for a double-hernia operation. More good laughs occur when the two wrestlers come out for the second fall, and Man Mountain Dean is afraid of Hugo. When Hugo's strength runs out, he still manages to win by accident, which is gratifying to the viewer. One of the funniest visuals during the wrestling match was a cutaway to the promoter (Eddie Kane) who raises his hat and yells "now" when he wants Hugo to win the fall. During the third fall, Kane is a scream as he keeps signaling louder and more aggressively until the cutaways from the match show him jumping, sweating, and yelling "NOW, NOW" to no avail. Even when compared to his much earlier wrestling scene which highlighted his earlier Warner Brothers movie *Sit Tight*, the comic bout in *The Gladiator* is superior.

Lucien Littlefield as the wacky Professor Danner delightfully recalls a similar character he played in Laurel and Hardy's *Dirty Work* when he enthusiastically creates a serum that can make old people young. Littlefield uses a lot of the same character traits from the earlier film as he creates the serum that turns Hugo into a superman.

After several films that pale in comparison to his movies at Warner Brothers, *The Gladiator* emerges as every bit as good as anything he'd done for that studio. It has a strong, consistent narrative, it is very funny, and it's also quite moving. Joe E. Brown turns in one of his best performances in one of his best roles. The reviews in the press, as well as in the trades, were strong, and audiences responded favorably as well. And it might be the best film to use when introducing a newbie to Joe E. Brown's films. His character is likeable, the slapstick is enjoyable and the narrative is accessible.

The Gladiator ended David Loew's two-picture distribution deal with Columbia Pictures, but Joe E. Brown had one more movie to make for the producer. Plans were for Brown to once again revisit his past work by making a comedy about a theatrical troop of which he's in charge. Loew managed to land a one-picture distribution deal with Metro-Goldwyn-Mayer which was quite prestigious, even if the studio was only handling that aspect of the movie and had nothing to do with its production. It meant the possibility of better bookings. So, plans were underway to begin shooting *Flirting With Fate*.

FLIRTING WITH FATE

Directed by Frank McDonald
Screenplay: Joseph Moncure March, Charlie Melson, Ethel La Blanche, Harry Clork from a story by Dan Jarrett and A. Dorian Otvos
Produced by David L Loew
Cinematography: George Schneiderman
Film Editing: Robert O. Crandall

Cast:
Joe E. Brown, Leo Carrillo, Beverly Roberts, Wynne Gibson, Steffi Duna, Charles Judels, Stanley Fields, Leonid Kinskey, Chris-Pin Martin, Inez Palange, Irene Franklin, Jay Novello, George Humbert, Lew Kelly, Phillip Trent, Ann Hovey, Dick Botiller, Carlos Villarias, Harry Semels, Charles Stevens

Released December 2, 1938
Running time: 69 minutes
David L. Loew productions for Metro-Goldwyn-Mayer
Black and White

Joe E. Brown's last movie for David Loew was more of a straight comedy with Brown playing a regular role rather than one that was tailored to his comic talents. While he adds elements of his established comedy to the character, it is much more a part of the organic narrative.

Joe plays Dan Dixon, head of an American entertainment troop traveling in South America for a gig. They are first confronted by a band of outlaws whose leader, Sancho Ramirez (Leo Carrillo), is attracted to the troop's dancer Carlita (Steffi Duna), so he does not rob or hurt anyone. The group then gets in a car accident with a furious man who is being chauffeured. Dan's attempts to extricate the man's car from the mud results in the man falling into the mud face first. When they get to their destination, Dan discovers that this irate man is Don Luis Garcia (Charles Judels), the theater owner who hired them. He is actually ready to forgive, but Dan's further bumbling ruins the opportunity. Things seem to improve when the troupe gets a shot at a Broadway show, with the understanding that Dan is not involved. He only reveals to the others of the Broadway opportunity, not that he isn't to be included. The situation, however, is challenging because they do not have the money to get back to the States. Despondent, Dan considers killing himself so the troupe can use the insurance money left behind. When he botches this, he tries to get himself into situations where he will get killed, so the troupe will have the same benefit. A drunken Dan confronts Sancho Ramirez in a café, but Sancho is stopped by Carlita. Dan then offers some of the insurance money to be killed, and Sancho agrees, inviting him to his hacienda to make these arrangements. There is a conflict between Sancho and one of his men, Fernando (Stanley Fields), that results in imprisonment that also includes Dan, and Don Luis Garcia, who is at the hacienda party by invitation to audition Carlita. Garcia offers Dan and his troupe a one-year contract if Dan can think of a way to get them out of jail. They escape by pretending that a bottle of water is nitro glycerin. Dan tosses away the bottle, and it explodes, as it actually was nitro glycerin.

Flirting With Fate is a rather offbeat movie for Joe E. Brown, and not a very good one. It is gratifying that Joe plays Dan Dixon as a confident, brave type in most situations, exhibiting a secure cockiness in the opening scenes. He is also a bumbler as per most of his Loew films, and it gets him, and his troupe, into trouble. There is some reference to a romance between Dan and Patricia Lane (Beverly Roberts), a member of his troupe, but it is never really explored. Most of the attention involves Dan's comic conflicts with Sancho or Don Luis.

There are a few highlights along the way. Joe does a delightful dance with Steffi Duna, and both Leo Carrillo and Charles Judels play amusing comic foils. The conclusion, when Brown and Judels don a bull suit and are not only pursued by a real bull, but attacked by a hornet's nest, is probably the funniest sequence. The troupe

An explosion leaves Beverly Roberts and Joe up a tree in Flirting With Fate

is given little to do, staying off screen for most of the movie, but they do save the day when they bring the police in the end. The final explosion, makes for a fun conclusion. The ensemble dynamic between Dan and the rest of the theatre troupe is interesting and different from the rest of his films, as he was actually in charge of this troupe. He has never before began a film in a position of power like that in many—if any—of his previous movies. It is also unfortunate that the romance wasn't given a lot of attention. It felt very lived in—they were already together at the beginning of the film, but the plot didn't affect their relationship specifically, so it didn't really go beyond that.

The part of the plot where Dan decided to kill himself to cash in on the life insurance has some similarity to his Warner misfire *A Very Honorable Guy*, only less morbid. Maybe that's partially why it wasn't as well-received.

Flirting With Fate is a pretty mild affair, perhaps not as bad as *When's Your Birthday* or *Riding on Air*, but not nearly as good as *The Gladiator*, or even *Wide Open Faces* or *Fit for a King*.

While Joe was promoting *Flirting With Fate*, he revealed one of his most noted character traits in an interview:

> A humorous happenstance led Joe E. Brown to adopt his trade mark, his famous "E-E-yow!" yell. The comedian revealed the source of his distinctive cry yes terday while discussing his new M.G.M. picture, *Flirting With Fate*. Fifteen years ago, he and a friend were sharing a beach cottage on the lake front at Toledo, O. Brown had difficulty every morning arousing his friend to go in swimming. On this particular occasion he had no luck at all and went swimming alone. He decided he should awaken his friend but didn't want to go back to the cottage. Instead he opened his mouth as wide as he could and let out a tremendous "E-E-yow!" His pal went right on sleeping, he said, but half-clad figures dashed from many of the other cottages. Amazed at the carrying power of the yell, Brown tried it out on his next audience and has used it ever since for a laugh.[63]

Critics and audiences were both underwhelmed by *Flirting With Fate*, with *The Brooklyn Daily Eagle* stating:

> Joe E. Brown doesn't need much material to make a screen comedy. He rarely gets more than he can use. But in *Flirting With Fate*, previewed yesterday at the Criterion Theater, he is practically destitute. Few jokes, fewer comic situations and no support. Fact is there is nothing to support, for Joe E. Brown is at low ebb. *Flirting With Fate* finds him leading his vaudeville troupe by trailer through the gaucho country, headed for Asuncion, Paraguay. His troubles start when he runs into Leo Carrillo, bandit, and tosses an immaculate Latin-American gentleman into a puddle of mud. The low comedy that follows, when Joe tries to commit suicide so that his troupe can get home on

---

63 Origin of Brown's "E-E-yow" Revealed. *The Los Angeles Times*. October 29, 1938

the proceeds from his insurance policy, is the work of six writers. Count them.[64]

Meanwhile, reports from exhibitors in the trades indicated that audiences weren't particularly amused by *Flirting With Fate* either, one theater owner stating that if Joe made many more like this, he might as well retire.

Flirting With Fate concluded Joe E. Brown's contract with David Loew and he was now free to seek work elsewhere. While in negotiation to make features for Columbia Pictures, who were pleased with the success of *The Gladiator*, Joe signed to do a one-shot film for Paramount Pictures. Martha Raye had recently emerged as the female large-mouthed counterpart to large-mouthed Joe, and arrangements were explored to team them up for a movie. Martha Raye was attached for a time to *The Gladiator*, and then later to this film. Neither of these situations worked out. So Martha Raye's own studio, Paramount Pictures, where she scored opposite W.C. Fields and Bob Hope in *The Big Broadcast of 1938*, came up with a vehicle for her to co-star with the newly available Joe E. Brown. Unfortunately, *$1000 A Touchdown*, is not worth either of their talents.

---

64 More New Films Have Local Premieres. *Brookly Daily Eagle* December 15, 1938

$1000 A TOUCHDOWN

Directed by James P. Hogan
Screenplay: Delmer Daves from his story
Produced by William C. Thomas
Cinematography: William Mellor
Film Editing: Chandler House

Cast:

Joe E. Brown, Martha Raye, Eric Blore, Susan Hayward, John Hartley Joyce Mathews, George McKay, Syd Saylor, Tom Dugan, Matt McHugh, Don Wilson, Arthur Bernard, Linda Brent, Don Evan Brown, Jack Chapin, Maxine Conrad, D'Arcy Corrigan, Dorothy Dayton, Paul DeCardo, John Hart, James Hogan, Judy King, Bob Layne, Patsy Mace, Wanda McKay, Adrian Morris, Constanine Romanoff, Jolly Rawlings, Jack Shea, Hugh Sothern, Hamilton McGlen Sr, Harry Templeton, Frank M. Thomas, Cheryl Walker, Jane Webb, Tiny Whitt, Emmett Vogan, Gertrude Astor, Dewey Robinson, Bill Thompson, Jack Perin, Charles Middleton, Johnnie Morris, William Haade, Dot Farley, Phil Dunham, Jimmy Conlin, Fritzi Brunette, George Barton, Grace Goodall, Edward Gargan.

Released Ocrober 4, 1939
Running time: 71 minutes
Paramount Pictures
Black and White

Free from his contract with David Loew, Joe E. Brown looked into several opportunities to ply his craft, be it stage performances, movies, or radio. During the 1938-1939 season, while waiting for his agent to secure another movie or theater contract, Joe E. Brown starred on his own radio show. It was a fun, wholesome show for children that was sponsored by Post Toasties cereal and performed

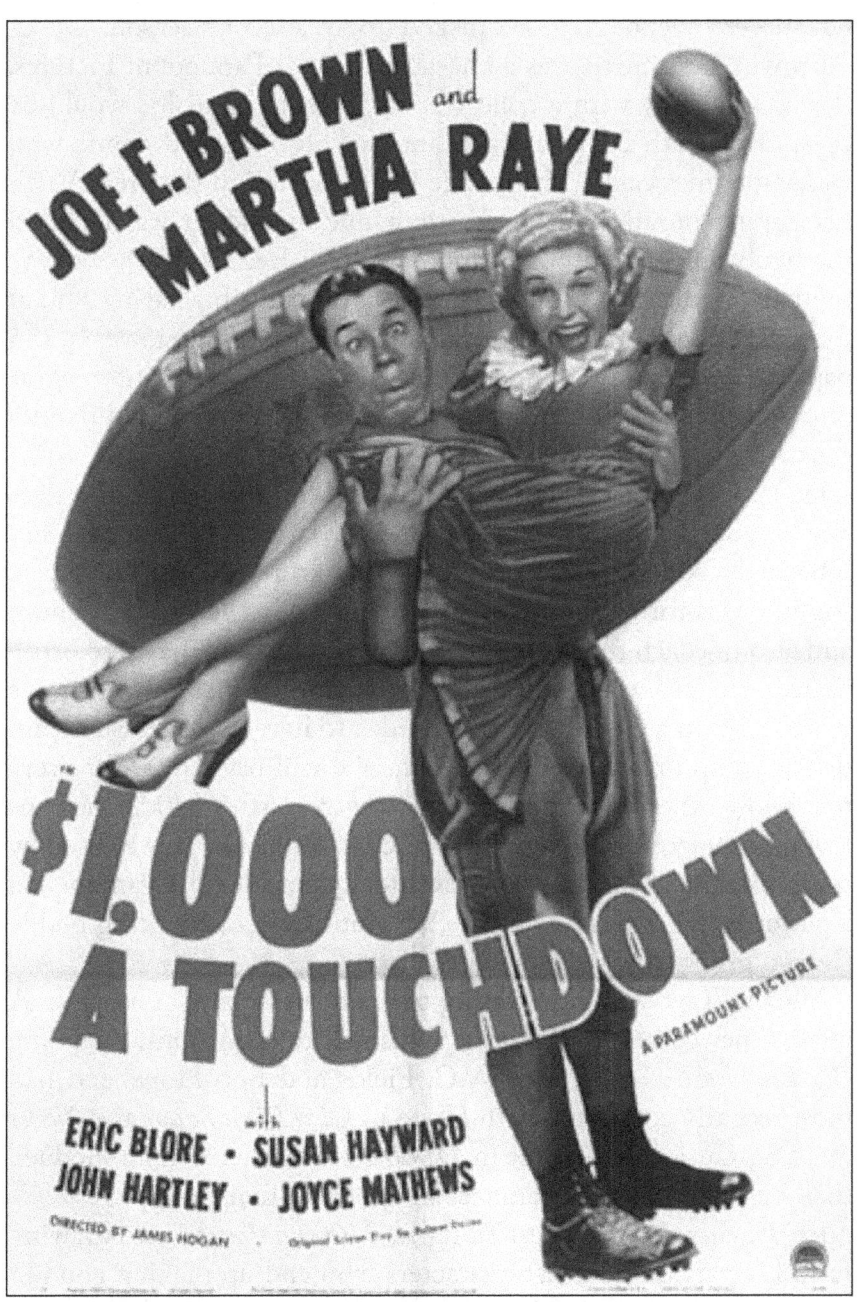

Ad for $1000 a Touchdown

for a live audience. However, despite good reviews, the show was not successful enough to get picked up for a second season.

Brown's next movie was a one-shot deal for Paramount Pictures. It was a comedy with a college football theme, and Joe would be co-starring with Martha Raye, another big-mouthed comic who was sometimes called "the female Joe E. Brown" in the press. With her gaping mouth and bombastic comic manner, it was believed the two would play off of each other nicely. Because of the college football premise, Joe was looking forward to possibly having a hit at the level of *The Gladiator*, which had been his best film in years. On paper, it looked like a winner. It was not. Even in his autobiography years later, Joe E. Brown looked back on this film and bluntly stated, "It was terrible!"

Joe E. Brown plays Marlowe Mansfield Smith, the son of a classically trained actor, and Martha Raye is Martha Madison, who has inherited a college that is ready to go bankrupt. Marlow has stage fright, but is thrust into the job of helping Martha run the college and also to coach the football team, even though he has zero experience. He has never even seen a game, nor does he know how it's played. Martha comes up with the idea to have her lackluster team play a group of professionals, whom she will pay $1000 for every touchdown they allow her players to score. After $4000 she runs low on money so she lowers the price to $100, but it is refused by the pro team. Marlowe must eventually get into the game when a player is injured, and wins the big game by actually being bodily thrown over the goal posts.

Martha Raye was just starting to make an impact in movies. A relative newcomer, Raye had a few small roles in films, including *Big Broadcast of 1938* with W.C. Fields and Bob Hope, and had most recently co-starred with Hope in *Give Me a Sailor* and *Never Say Die*. Curiously, her role in *$1000 a Touchdown* is more subdued than her bombastic appearances in the other films.

Joe E. Brown is the best thing in *$1000 a Touchdown*, drawing from his past milquetoast characters who end up making good in the end. However, in this film, Joe's character doesn't suddenly understand the game or learn as he attempts to coach. He wins the game on a fluke done with a purely a mechanical gag. Still, Joe

Joe and Martha Raye couldn't save the weak script for $1000 a Touchdown

remains appealing, utilizing what works and doing what he can with the thin material. The movie is filled with great old veterans like Jimmy Conlin, Matt McHugh, and Eric Blore with whom Joe had worked so successfully in *Sons o' Guns*. But they can't overcome the lackluster material either.

There is even further historical interest in *$1000 a Touchdown* because it features an early performance by Susan Hayward, who went on to an award-winning career as a major motion picture star. Hayward plays a lovesick student who writes poetry, and doesn't make too much of an impact overall, but because of her later stardom, there is some interest in that it is an early appearance of hers.

The outrageous script for *$1000 a Touchdown* is by Delmer Daves who is now considered a great screenwriter and director, responsible for such films as *Destination Tokyo, Pride of the Marines, Dark Passage, The Last Wagon, 3:10 to Yuma, The Badlanders,* and *Spencer's Mountain*. Regarding comedy, Daves had just written *Professor Beware* for Harold Lloyd, also a Paramount release, and a comparatively weaker film for that great star. Director Frank McDonald had most recently been helming films in the Bulldog Drummond series, and had little background in comedy.

Paramount did its best to market this teaming of Joe E. Brown and Martha Raye, including involving Joe's radio sponsor, Post

Joe is an unlikely college football coach in $1000 a Touchdown

Toasties cereal. The studio completed a national advertising tie-up with Post Toasties with both Joe, and Martha, featured in a series of three 800-liine newspaper ads plugging both the breakfast food and the movie, appearing in leading key cities. And at a theater in Georgia, the owner secured the cooperation of the local high school football team which paraded the streets of Vidalia, stopping along the way to perform plays like punting, passing, etc. Banners with the movie's title and play dates were displayed.

Unfortunately, the cleverness of these promotional ideas did not result in a very good box office response. When the film played theaters, disappointed patrons from its opening night would let others know that the movie was not very good.

The fact that *$1000 a Touchdown* was such a disappointment really affected Joe E. Brown's film career. He had already gone from top box office star at a major studio, to a series of generally substandard indie productions, and now a flop that caused exhibitors and critics to sadly admit his days as a star were finished. Frank S. Nugent stated in *The New York Times*:

> Paramount must have been carried away when it finally succeeded in bringing Joe E. Brown and Martha Raye

(and their mouths) together in a comedy. Only it wasn't carried far enough away. *$1,000 a Touchdown* is a painfully witless football farce of almost fantastic unoriginality. There is even a scene in which Eric Blore turns to Mr. Brown and says, "Now I leave you to Morpheus." It ends with Joe E. scoring the last-second touchdown by being thrown over the goal posts. They threw the wrong man: Delmer Daves, who wrote it, would be our choice—and we'd insist on a field goal.

$1000 a Touchdown performed poorly at the box office, playing the second half of double bill programs in neighborhood theaters.

Despite his career doldrums, Joe E. Brown managed to secure a contract to make features at Columbia pictures. Although it was part of the B unit, Columbia head Harry Cohn liked Joe and believed his name still held enough box office clout for a starring comedy series. Columbia had distributed Joe's last few Loew productions, and had a hit with *The Gladiator*. Thus, his first film under the new contract planned to reunite him with that film's director, Edward Sedgwick. Also, *Beware Spooks* would feature a screenplay by Richard Flournoy, who had penned *Riding on Air*, *Fit for a King*, and *Wide Open Faces*, and had been currently writing the popular *Blondie* series of films at Columbia. Joe E. Brown hoped to rescue his flagging movie career.

BEWARE SPOOKS!

Directed by Edward Sedgwick
Screenplay: Richard Flournay, Albert Duffy, and Brian Marlow based on Flournoy's play
Produced by Robert Sparks
Cinematography: Allen Siegler
Film Editing: James Sweeney

Cast:
Joe E. Brown, Mary Carlisle, Clarence Kolb, Marc Lawrence, Don Beddoe, George J. Lewis, James Blaine, Jack Egan, Frank M. Thomas, Howard Hickman, Charles lane, Iris Meredith, Cy Schindell, Lorna Gray, Frank Moran, Stanley Mack, Robert B. Williams, Walter Sande, Joe Palma, Al Rhein, Stanley Mack, Claire Rochelle, Pat McKee, Al Rhein, George McKay, Ethelreda Leopold, Edythe Elliot, Eddie Laughton, Byron Foulger, Dickie Jones.

Released October 24, 1939
Running time: 65 minutes
Columbia Pictures
Black and White

For his first film under his contract with Columbia Pictures, Joe E. Brown appears to have made his peace with the screen persona he had developed since leaving Warner Brothers. Despite the success of *The Gladiator* a year earlier, it was perhaps believed that, as he neared 50, Joe was no longer believable as the swaggering athlete brimming with small town confidence. Instead, he appears to have decided to embrace the role of the comic bumbler who earnestly tries to make good and emerges triumphant at the end.

This formula would be essentially his basis for the remainder of his starring comedies. As Joe E. Brown approached the 1940s,

Ad for Beware Spooks, *Joe's first film on a new Columbia Pictures contract*

other factors got in the way of his movie career, and other ideas were explored. Joe's best screen work would remain from 1931-1936. However, at Columbia, Joe E. Brown, at the very least, did enjoy some minor success once he settled into the status of a bumbling B movie comic that offered a 65 minute warmup to the main feature.

Beware Spooks! features Joe E. Brown as Roy Gifford, a typical bumbler who follows in his successful father's footsteps as a member of the police force. The problem is, Roy is so inept, he actually helps crimes happen rather than thwart them. The underworld is quite pleased with Roy, and he garners something of a reputation. When he is on duty, crimes are easily committed, often with his unwitting assistance. However, when he allows the notorious public enemy Slick Eastman (Marc Lawrence) to slip through his fingers, Roy is fired from the police force. Despondent, Roy takes his wife Betty Lou (Mary Carlisle) on a honeymoon to Coney Island to get away from his troubles. However, while there, he spots Slick Eastman and decides to capture him to clear his name and reputation. This results in a long chase through the funhouse at the amusement park.

While it utilizes around 15 of its 65 minutes on the climactic slapstick chase scene that concludes the film, *Beware Spooks!* is pretty slow going until that wild finish. There is a lot of character development, and the plot exposition consists of scenes where Roy's ineptitude is presented. Clarence Kolb is quite funny as the

Marc Lawrence, Joe E. Brown, and Clarence Kolb in Beware Spooks

irate police commissioner, Marc Lawrence is perfectly cast as the tough talking gangster, and Mary Carlisle always manages to hold her own when supporting comedians. There is a fun scene with Roy and Betty Lou in their hotel room with Roy's awkward fumbling, and Betty Lou was a good lead female character in the way she took initiative to follow the crooks and help Roy capture them.

There is a general pleasantness to the proceedings and it is much more amusing and disarming than most of the David Loew productions. And although it is shot for Columbia's B unit, the budget is much better. In fact, an entire Coney Island set on the Columbia backlot was used.

> Famed Coney Island, with all its color and gayety, has been constructed at the Columbia Ranch in San Fernando Valley for the Joe E. Brown comedy, *Beware Spooks!* The setting, covering several acres, includes a part of the world-famed boardwalk, merry-go-round, Ferris wheel, chute-the-chutes and numerous concessions typical of the midway. The scenes are being filmed at night and the

setting is a picturesque panorama of multicolored lights, crowds, barkers hawkers and mechanical amusements in full blast.[65]

It is the climactic chase scene where *Beware Spooks!* really comes to life and never really lets up. In fact, it is such a fast-paced sequence, and lasts so long, it allows one to forget how slow the exposition had been in order to reach the wild finish. They use the intricacies of the set and all the opportunities that the funhouse attractions present them to create some really funny and fast-paced slapstick.

So, *Beware Spooks* is a pleasant and disarming experience that picks up and becomes raucously hilarious slapstick as it ends. It can be argued that, other than *The Gladiator*, it features Joe E. Brown's finest performance since leaving Warner Brothers. He seems rejuvenated now that he was under contract to a new studio, and away from the doldrums of the Loew productions.

During the filming of *Beware Spooks*, Joe E. Brown was allowed some time off to see the final two days of a baseball tournament:

> Joe E. Brown Jr., who has been willed, by his father, the largest individually owned collection of sports souvenirs, with the understanding that they eventually pass into possession of the Toledo, Ohio, Museum, will have another souvenir added to his collection Monday afternoon when the final game of the Oakland Tribune State Championship Tournament will be played at the Oaks' Ball Park. The screen comedian, who will make his first appearance here Sunday at The Tribune games, has made it a hobby of collecting some sort of trinket from all sports events he attends, but he never has received an autographed baseball symbolic of the California State semi-pro championship. It was while making the picture *Beware Spooks!* that the Columbia screen star announced his pleasure to attend the State title play-offs here Sunday and Monday, and that he would turn all his souvenirs over to his son. The reason for Brown requesting his son to eventually turn the sou-

---

65 Coney Island Used in New Comedy. *Rochester Democrat and Chronicle.* September 18, 1939

venirs over to the Toledo Museum is that he was born at Holgate, a little town just outside of Toledo. Included in the collection of souvenirs are autographed baseballs from almost every World Series, the shoes worn by James Braddock when he won the world's heavyweight title, scores of autographed footballs and a wealth of mementoes from memorable sporting events.[66]

Joe E. Brown returned to filming after this two day absence, and the movie was brought in on time and within its budget.

Reviews for *Beware Spooks!* were mixed. Some called it a return to form for Joe E. Brown, proclaiming it his best in some time. Others dismissed it as dull, trite, and that the fun climax was little more than mechanical gags. Exhibitors reporting in the trades were equally mixed in response to *Beware Spooks!* Some indicated it played to packed houses that laughed uproariously throughout the film. Others indicated that the film drew poorly and audiences were underwhelmed.

The truth lies somewhere in-between. The general pleasantness of *Beware Spooks!* and the wild slapstick conclusion result in an overall average movie, that is not a highlight in Joe E. Brown's career, nor is it a misfire. It likely ranks alongside the recent *Fit for a King*, which was mildly enjoyable with some good scenes.

Still, Joe E. Brown was ready to work hard and make his Columbia output as close to the level of his Warner Brothers successes. Columbia, realizing what had worked with his first film at their studio, placed Joe in another gangster comedy. *So You Won't Talk* was to be shot after the 1939 holidays in early 1940. However, before the holidays happened, Joe E. Brown was involved in a serious auto crash where he narrowly escaped being killed.

---

66 TOURNEY VICTOR TO GIVE JOE E. BROWN SOUVENIR Film Comedian, Owner of Largest Sport Collection, to See Final Two Days of Play. *Oakland Tribune.* August 31, 1939.

SO YOU WON'T TALK

Directed by Edward Sedgwick
Screenplay: Richard Flournay
Produced by Robert Sparks
Cinematography: Allen Siegler
Film Editing: James Sweeney

Cast:
Joe E. Brown, Frances Robinson, Bibienne Osborne, Bernard Nedell, Tom Dugan, Dick Wessel, Anthony Warde, Don Beddoe, Helen Troy, Jack Byron, Sam Bernard, Harry Anderson, Evelyn Young, Frank Milan, Eddie Acuff, Luis Alberni, Stanley Andrews Bruce Bennett, Wade Boteler, Chick Chandler, Jimmy Conlin, Richard Fiske, Harrison Greene, Jack Norton, Walter Sande, Ralph Sanford Cy Schindell, Charles C. Wilson, Eddie Coke, Jackie Egan, M.J. Frankovich, George Hickman, Walter Lawrence, William Lally, Eddie Laughton, George McKay, James Milllican, Charles R. Moore, Helen Troy.

Released October 3, 1940
Running time: 69 minutes
Columbia Pictures
Black and White

Joe E. Brown was preparing to begin work on the second film in his Columbia contract, when on December 5, 1939 he was involved in a serious car accident. Joe could have been preoccupied in that his daughter, Kathryn, had recently been thrown from a horse and was in the hospital with a fractured skull (the child fully recovered and is still alive at the time of this writing). According to a press account:

> Film Comedian Joe E. Brown grinned tonight and suggested that doctors might as well sew up part of his wide

mouth while they stitched his lip, injured when the actor's station wagon crashed with an automobile and rolled 30 feet down an embankment. Police expressed amazement that Brown escaped with his life. The machine he was driving side-swiped a car driven by Charles E. Weaver of Montrose, and careened wildly for 275 feet before leaving the road. The accident occured in front of the home of Jane Withers, juvenile actress, and her mother was the first to reach Brown. "Don't move me," the comedian mumbled to Mrs. Withers. "Please call my wife and a doctor." She did and Brown was removed to California Lutheran hospital where physicians gave him treatment. One of Brown's first concerns then was whether he would be allowed to see the Coast conference championship football game Saturday. "I'll see that game no matter what happens," Brown promised. The accident was the third misfortune in a string of bad luck for the Brown family. A seven-year-old daughter, Kathryn Brown, is in the same hospital recovering from a skull fracture received in a fall from a horse recently. Joe Jr. is wearing his arm in a sling for a fractured arm received In a U.C.L.A. basketball game. The driver of the other car in the traffic accident suffered only minor cuts.[67]

However, it appears the news story was not very forthcoming as to the seriousness of Joe E. Brown's injuries. He suffered a collapsed lung and was put in a full body cast. He not only missed the football game, he spent Christmas in the hospital.

Joe E. Brown had become quite active since finishing work on *Beware Spooks!*, including getting involved at a political level. Joe flew to Washington to speak in favor of allowing Jewish refugee children into the United States. It is an unfortunate part of American history that this was not a popular idea at the time. Brown was among the few notable Americans to speak on behalf of these children. The bill did not pass, and it is likely at least some of these children ended up in concentration camps.

---

67 Joe E. Brown Hurt in Hollywood Accident. *Bakersfield Califorina.* December 6, 1936

Tom Dugan and Joe in So You Won't Talk

There were plans for Joe to do a stage act between pictures, recalling some of his old vaudeville bits, and he was to participate in a stage revival of one of his biggest theater hits, *Elmer The Great*, which was also, of course, a hit movie. Instead, Joe spent a lot of time laid up, pondering where he wanted to go with his career, taking stock of decisions, good and bad, to result in his current status. Fortunately, like his daughter, Joe E. Brown did recover from the car crash and was able to start work on his next movie, *So You Won't Talk* in the summer of 1940.

In 1935, Columbia released a John Ford film called *The Whole Town's Talking* where Edward G. Robinson played a dual role. He was a shy, easily-intimidated office worker, and a snarling notorious gangster. The comedy comes from the two identical men being mistaken for each other. The main gag was noted gangster actor Robinson also playing the withdrawn, reserved type. *So You Won't Talk* is remarkably similar to the John Ford movie. Joe E. Brown plays dual roles, the bearded intellectual "Whiskers," and the gangster Brute Hanson, who has just been released from prison. The plot has Whiskers being fired from his newspaper job. He shaves his beard, which makes him a dead ringer for the gangster. Unlike the Edward G. Robinson performance, *So You Won't Talk* is amusing because of Brown's portrayal of the gangster, which is against type for him. Not only is Joe's turn as the snarling gangster amusing, it works well because Brown was actually convincing in that sort of role. He was able to change his facial expressions and his manner of speaking just enough to make it work, and to make the gangster a distinct character from Whiskers.

So You Won't Talk has the same overall disarming pleasantness as *Beware Spooks!* had. It is fun to see Joe call up his old milquetoast role that had served him well in Warner movies like *Local Boy Makes Good*. And there are a lot of elements that make *So You Won't Talk* an amusing experience. Whiskers not only has to deal with Brute's own gang members and moll taking umbrage at his inability to recognize them, he also has to deal with another gangster who is intent on killing him.

Dick Wessell and Anthony Warde are fun as Brute's bumbling henchmen Dopey and Dolf, while Vivienne Osborne plays her part as Brute's moll quite well. Frances Robinson is an attractive presence as Whiskers' girl Lucy, and Bernard Nedell is nicely menacing as Brute's rival Bugs Linaker. As with *Beware Spooks!*, *So You Won't Talk* is an amusing trifle that is better than most of his Loew productions but not as good as his Warner efforts.

At least one newspaper article was impressed at how well Joe bounced back from his serious accident:

> Joe E. Brown's first week before the cameras in *So You Won't Talk*, marking his return to the screen after a serious automobile accident that put him in the hospital for four months, left no doubt that he was fully recovered. In the first three days Joe fell off beds, crawled under them, jumped out of a second-story window, and swung a haymaker to Charles Wilson's jaw that connected accidentally and knocked the actor senseless for two minutes.[68]

This was Joe E. Brown's only movie to be released in 1940, and he was off screen for all of 1941. There were rumblings that America

---

68 Vale, Virginia. Star Dust column. *Western Newspaper Union*. July 17, 1940

may end up joining the war in Europe, and the Brown family contributed patriotically. Joe's sons Don and Joe jr. were enlisted in the air force. His wife was active in the local Red Cross.

Joe himself began entertaining at various military bases, enjoying the immediacy of a live audience. He also returned to the theater in the *Elmer The Great* revival that was held back until he was healed from his injuries and once again available. He also remained political, speaking against the Japanese internment camps, which was, amazingly, not a popular opinion at the time. It was not until 1942 before another Joe E. Brown movie was in theaters, and by that time America was involved in a second World War and Joe was even more interested in entertaining the troops.

SHUT MY BIG MOUTH

Directed by Charles Barton
Screenplay: Oliver Drake, Karen DeWolf, Francis Martin from a story by Drake
Produced by Robert Sparks
Cinematography: Henry Freulich
Film Editing: Gene Havlick

Cast:
Joe E. Brown, Adele Mara, Victory Jory, Fritz Feld, Don Beddoe, Will Wright, Russell SImopson, Joan Woodbury Lloyd Bridges Ralph Peters, Joe McGuinn, Forrest Tucker, Pedro de Cordoba, Noble Johnson, Chief Thundercloud, Iron Eyes Cody, Dick Curtis, Art Mix, Bob Folkerson, Al Ferguson, Blackjack Ward, Clay DeRoy, Blackie Whitford, Lew Kelly, Edward Peil sr, John Tyrrell, Art Dillard, Eddy Waller, Georgia Backus, J.W. Cody, Hank Bell, Earl Hodgins, Ray Jones.

Released February 19, 1942
Running time: 71 minutes
Columbia Pictures
Black and White

The year 1941 was the first since 1927 where no Joe E. Brown movie was in release. During that year, movie comedy changed. The folksy humor of Joe E. Brown belonged very much to the 1930s, while the brash, fast-talking comedy of Bob Hope and Abbott and Costello were better representative of the new decade. However, there was still room for the type of homespun slapstick that Joe E. Brown was now performing in B movies that supported double-bills and played to neighborhood theaters. Often children were the main audience demographic.

Ad for Shut My Big Mouth, *one of Joe's best Columbia releases*

It is frequently stated in other studies that *Shut My Big Mouth* was Joe E. Brown's comeback vehicle after the late 1939 auto accident, but actually newspaper accounts indicate that *So You Won't Talk* was the first movie he filmed after his recovery. Shooting began on that film in the early summer of 1940 for release at the end of that year.

Shut My Big Mouth is a western comedy in which Joe E. Brown plays an Eastern horticulturist named Wellington Holmes who is traveling with his valet Robert Oglethorpe (Fritz Feld). Their intention is to beautify the west by planting colorful flowers. When their stagecoach is held up en route by masked bandit Buckskin Bill (Victor Jory) and his gang (Forrest Tucker, Lloyd Bridges), Holmes accidentally thwarts the robbery when he faints and pulls down a bunch of potted plants from the roof of the Stagecoach onto the bandits. The drivers of the coach look down and see the bandits have been subdued and are impressed with Holmes' courage and skill. Just then a posse of townspeople ride up and are so impressed, Holmes is made their new Marshall. When his plans to sneak away fail, Holmes must somehow go along with the situation, calling himself a "lone wolf" so that others are not around when he

Joe and Fritz Feld in Shut My Big Mouth

attempts to battle bandits, and he can sneak away and return East. In one effort to escape, Holmes dresses like a woman and pretends to be Oglethorpe's wife. However, they get caught up in a kidnapping when Buckskin Bill captures Don Carlos Montoya (Pedro de Cordoba), the father of pretty Elena (Adele Mara) to whom Holmes is attracted. Holmes later inadvertently subdues Buckskin Bill and his gang once again but Bill is without his mask and thus disguised as one of his gang. Imprisoned, he agrees to lead the others to Buckskin Bill, not revealing it is really him. When they arrive at the hideout, Holmes sneaks into a room, dons a dress, and again pretends to be Mrs. Oglethorpe. However, his dress catches fire and his disguise is revealed. He escapes, throws his burning dress into a haystack, and the smoke alerts a group of Indians whom Holmes had earlier befriended. They come to his rescue.

As with Joe E. Brown's other Columbia comedies, *Shut My Big Mouth* benefits from a general pleasantness that permeates the entire film. But this one is especially fast paced and amusing with several good comic highlights.

Joe's scenes in drag as Mrs. Oglethorpe provide some of the movie's biggest laughs. He he calls up his dancing skills in a scene where Buckskin Bill dances with Holmes as Mrs. Oglethorpe, believing the disguise. The dance evolves into the two engaging in a raucous, slapstick-filled battle. There are some good laughs when the maid Maria (Joan Woodbury) is told to undress Mrs. Oglethorpe and put her to bed. Holmes realizes undressing will be embarrass-

Victor Jory and Joe share a laugh in Shut My Big Mouth

ingly revealing, so he battles and dodges Maria's attempts, while she believes Mrs. Oglethorpe is just bashful. Holmes finally gets away when he is unfazed by a mouse crawling on his arm, but a frightened Maria faints.

It is during one of his escape attempts when Holmes is confronted by an Indian tribe. Dressed in male cowboy gear but sporting the wig he uses when disguised as Mrs. Oglethorpe, Holmes agrees to scalp himself, and cuts a piece of the wig away. The Indians are so impressed, they make him a blood brother. This leads to their appearance later in the film where they rescue him.

The two big scenes where Holmes subdues the bandits are fast-paced and fun, buoyed by the direction of Charles Barton, who would later direct some of the better Abbott and Costello vehicles like *The Time of Their Lives*, *Africa Screams*, and *Abbott and Costello Meet Frankenstein*. The slapstick proceedings offer as much excitement as laughter.

Joe disguises himself as a woman in Shut My Big Mouth

Shut My Big Mouth benefits from a strong cast, including the aforementioned Feld, Jory, Tucker, Bridges, Mara, and Woodbury, but also such familiar faces as Will Wright, Don Beddoe, and Iron Eyes Cody. Western movie villains like Dick Curtis and Art Mix, who had appeared as cowboy heavies in Columbia films with Charles Starrett as The Durango Kid, add further cinematic authenticity.

A western comedy was a good idea at this point in Joe E. Brown's film career. Westerns had become very popular with the younger set, and that demographic had always been a strong factor regarding the success of Brown's work. So, during the era where Gene Autry, Roy Rogers, Tim Holt, The Durango Kid, and Hopalong Cassidy were enjoying popularity in neighborhood theaters, kids were treated to a comedy western featuring Joe.

By the time he made *Shut My Big Mouth*, he had been a B movie actor longer than he was a top box office attraction, and had firmly settled into that niche. Often when this film played the bottom half of a double bill, it was paired with a very big movie that could have likely stood alone, such as Walt Disney's *Dumbo* or John Ford's *How Green Was My Valley*. Thus, *Shut My Big Mouth* was less a companion feature and more of a warmup film. When it played in the neighborhood houses, it would invariably be paired with a B western, as the program's comedy relief.

Whatever the marketing choices might have been, *Shut My Big Mouth* was Joe E. Brown's best received feature since *The Gladiator* four years earlier. The trade magazine *Photoplay* had a rather philosophical approach in their review of the film:

> It's Joe E. Brown, folks, so what do you care if the story is a silly one about a wealthy horticulturist who goes out west with his valet, Fritz Feld, to beautify the desert? What do you care if Joe is forced to become a Marshall, then flee the unwanted job as a woman, and is later adopted by an Indian tribe, then tries to rescue the father of the girl he admires? What do you care as long as Joe E. Brown opens his mouth and makes you laugh? Shut up and laugh![69]

Heavily involved in the entertaining of troops at various army bases, even moreso now that America was involved in a second world war, Joe E. Brown didn't realize that his career as a starring comedian was coming to an end. In fact, his next Columbia comedy would not only fulfill his contract with that studio, it would conclude his series of starring comedies written and produced for his talents. He would lend support to hillbilly comedian Judy Canova for a couple of features at Republic studios, then play it fairly straight in two more movies before the 1940s were up, but *The Daring Young Man* would be Joe E. Brown's final starring comedy.

Because his Columbia contract was nonexclusive, Joe agreed to appear in a film with hillbilly comic Judy Canova at Republic Pictures.

---

69 Shut My Big Mouth review. *Photoplay*. March, 1942

JOAN OF OZARK

Directed by Joseph Santley
Screenplay: Jack Townley, Robert Harari and Eve Greene
Produced by Harriet Parsons
Cinematography: Ernest Miller
Film Editing: Charles Craft

Songs
Backwoods Barbecue
Lyrics by Mort Greene
Music by Harry Revel

Pull the Trigger
Lyrics by Mort Greene
Music by Harry Revel

Lady from Lockheed
Lyrics by Mort Greene
Music by Harry Revel

Cast:
Judy Canova, Joe E. Brown, Eddie Foy Jr, Jerome Cowan, Alexander Granach, Anne Jeffreys, Otto Reichow, Donald Curtis, Wolfgang Zilzer, Hans Heinrich von Twardowski, Harry Hayden, Wilhelm von Brincken, George Eldredge, Paul Fung, Gladys Gale, Tyler Gibosn, Nora Lane, Charles Miller, Bill Nestel, William Sundholm, Laura Treadwell, Lloyd Whitlock, William Worthington, Peppy and Peanuts Walters, Joan Tours, Pearl Tolson, Helen Seamon, Jean O'Connell, Ruby Morie, Aileen Morris, Billie Lane, Kay Gordon, Mary Jo Ellis, Jeanette Dickson, Jean Earle, Barbara Clark, Jane Allen Sally Carns, Patsy Bedell Eleanor Bailey, Audene Brier, Maxine Ardell, Eric Alden, Horace Carpenter, Emmett Lynn, Chester Clute, Midgie Dare, Robert Cherry, Pate Gleason, Ernest Hilliard, Olin Howland,

Bud Jamison, Johnny Luther, Ralph McCullogh, Tex Phelps, Cyril Ring, Ralph Peters, Bert Moorhouse, Jason Robards Sr, Bobby Stone, Kam Tong, Charles Williams.

Released July 15, 1942
Running time: 82 minutes
Republic Pictures
Black and White

Joan of Ozark isn't a Joe E. Brown movie at all. He is merely acting as a supporting player for the film's star, Judy Canova. Judy had established herself as a Hillbilly singer and comedian and in 1940 she began starring in low budget comedies for Republic Pictures. Known mostly for its westerns, Republic's films were so low on the studio wrung, they didn't even get reviewed in most of the major newspapers. Their movies were popular, especially those featuring singing cowboys Gene Autry or Roy Rogers, but they'd usually play neighborhood theaters as part of a double feature program.

Canova's films were rural comedies that appealed to a lot of moviegoers who also liked westerns, including children who had been the prime demographic for Joe E. Brown's films. And now that Joe E. Brown was long past his time as a Top Ten box office movie star, a low budget studio like Republic Pictures could afford his services. Thus, adding Joe to the cast of Judy's latest movie was a good marketing strategy.

Judy Canova had enjoyed some popularity at Republic already, starring in tailor-made vehicles with titles like *Scatterbrain* (1940) and *Puddin' Head* (1941). Joseph Santley, who started out directing Vitaphone musical shorts, helmed most of Canova's comedies at Republic.

By the time she made *Joan of Ozark*, Judy Canova had secured enough popularity with rural moviegoers to warrant a syndicated profile:

> This is the real story of Judy Canova a poor little hillbilly girl who doesn't know her way around Hollywood and New York at all — and cows have wings! The Lynn Fontanne of the Everglades had just completed a two weeks'

Ad for Joan of Ozark, *first of a few films Joe made for Republic Pictures*

engagement at the Strand on Broadway and was preparing to depart on a tour of the army posts when I found her at the Warwick. So I said to this Jenny Lind of the Ozarks I said "Miss Canova how did you first become identified with corn?" Miss Canova replied: 'When I was a little girl in Jacksonville Fla my sister and I used to pick names out of the telephone book and we'd call them up and talk to them in a hayseed voice passing ourselves off as nieces or relatives come for a visit and why hadn't we been met at the depot? We had them crazy We did this so much that our mother got after us for it but from those kid pastimes came an idea to groom the corn in a big way and we did We did skits on Florida radio stations always crooning the corn songs pining for the Ozarks which I have never seen and singing the old hillbilly songs until eventually I became known as the Sara Bernhardt of the south, and went on from there to the stage and pictures. I'm with Republic now and my newest picture, *Joan of Ozark*, is to be released in a few weeks." Miss Canova somewhere along the dim dusty train to stardom learned to yodel — a "must" in hillbilly lore.[70]

Judy Canova's penchant for yodeling and Joe E. Brown's big mouthed yell seemed like a good pairing to all involved.

Canova plays nightclub singer Judy Hull who accidentally shoots down a pigeon and discovers it was carrying a message being sent by a Nazi spy ring hiding out in America. She is hailed as a hero and gets some publicity. This unnerves nightclub owner Phillip Munson (Jerome Cowan), who is secretly the head of the spy ring. Joe E. Brown plays Cliff Little, who, with his partner Eddie McCabe (Eddy Foy Jr), wants to promote a new young dancer named Marie Lamont (Anne Jeffreys). Munson pretends that the publicity Judy is getting has attracted him as a nightclub owner, and states that if Cliff and Eddie are able to deliver Judy to him, he will also put Marie on the bill. In fact, Munson plans to murder Judy as a lesson to any Americans who might be inspired by her actions. However,

---

70 Tucker, George. Pictures of Manhattan. Syndicated wire service. August 27, 1942.

Joe was now a B-movie actor, supporting Judy Canova in Joan of Ozark

when Judy becomes a big hit at the club and raises its box office revenue, the spies may have to rethink their plan.

As this is not a Joe E. Brown movie, it can't really be assessed as to how it responds to the rest of his filmography. Our approach can only be based on how effectively he plays his supporting role while Judy Canova stars. Joe is a co-star with ample screen time, but it is she who is central to the narrative. It is she who thwarts the Nazi spies. This pairing certainly worked better than Brown's with Martha Raye (even though his role in *$1000 a Touchdown* was definitely more of a leading role). Overall, it's a ridiculous bit of war propaganda but, as he did in his early roles when he wasn't fully the lead yet, Joe still makes an impact.

Joan of Ozark is one of Judy Canova's more enjoyable movies, using her rube character nicely and spotlighting her talents with songs and comic situations that respond best to her persona. And Joe's status as co-star, does mean his character gets involved in her various situations, using his own comic skills to enhance each scene. *Film Daily* understood the movie's appeal with their review:

> With Judy Canova and Joe E. Brown fans to draw upon, *Joan of Ozark* should make the grade nicely as family entertainment. Those two names spell slapstick comedy

and that is exactly what the customers get in generous helpings. It is a screwy comedy broader than Joe's mouth. That the story is one of those preposterous affairs that can't stand too close investigation will no doubt make no difference to the Canova-Brown fans. Nor is it likely that they will be disturbed by the fact that the humor, for the most part, is far from fresh and strictly routine.[71]

Judy Canova's popularity with rural audiences pretty much guaranteed this movie would be well received in those areas. But adding Joe E. Brown, who also remained quite popular with rural audiences, added greater strength to its box office success. Republic Pictures was very pleased with the results, and signed Joe to do two more movies with Judy Canova once he completed his Columbia contract. Joe liked working with Judy and welcomed the opportunity.

However, before starting production on his final movie for Columbia, Joe E. Brown made several appearances entertaining the troops.

---

71 Joan of Ozark review. *Film Daily.* July 15, 1942

THE DARING YOUNG MAN

Directed by Frank Strayer
Screenplay: Karen DeWolf, Connie Lee
Produced by Robert Sparks
Cinematography: Franz Planer
Film Editing: Al Clark

Cast:
Joe E. Brown, Marguerite Chapman, William Wright, Roger Clark, Claire Dodd, Lloyd Bridges, Donald Douglas, Frank Sully, Ben Carter, Eddie Laughton, Robert Emmett Keane, William Forrest, Robert Middlemass, Phil Van Zandt, Charles Wagenheim, Irving Bacon, Sam McDaniel, George Pembroke, Eddie Bruce, Jack Gardner, Nora Cecil, Lee Phelps, Hal Price, Ben Taggart, Minerva Urecal, Ben Taggart, Jean Inness, Edward McWade, Eddie Coke.

Released October 8, 1942
Running time: 73 minutes
Columbia Pictures
Black and White

The Daring Young Man concluded Joe E. Brown's contract with Columbia Pictures and is also the end of his starring comedy features. As indicated earlier, comedy had changed to a brasher, less folksy style that fit Bob Hope but not so much Joe E Brown. Interestingly, for his final Columbia feature, Joe worked with the team that had been making the studio's popular Blondie series. The producer, the director, and the screenwriters (notably both female) were the same team that had been responsible for the Blondie movies whose characters were based on Chic Young's comic strip.

Joe and Marguerite Chapman in The Daring Young Man, *Joe's last film on his Columbia contract*

Joe E Brown plays Jonathan Peckinpaw who owns a struggling air conditioning store, and lives there with his elderly grandmother (also played by Joe). Nazi spies bomb the store adjacent to Jonathan's and his business is destroyed. He attempts to enlist in every branch of the service, but is consistently turned down. Ann Minter (Marguerite Chapman), a pretty reporter Jonathan meets when she is covering the explosion, suggests he take up bowling to build up his strength. Jonathan is terrible at it, but Sam Long (William Wright), an enterprising inventor, rigs his shortwave machine to a ball so that it gets a strike no matter how poorly Jonathan throws it. It works, and Jonathan, with Long's help, earns a lot of money with contests and endorsements. Long even charges kids a dime each to get Jonathan's autograph. The Nazi spies who blew up the building housing Jonathan's store discover that Long's machine is interrupting their attempts to send short wave signals to their comrades. They befriend Jonathan and Sam Long, and drug them in an effort to find out more about their shortwave system, but are not successful. Later,

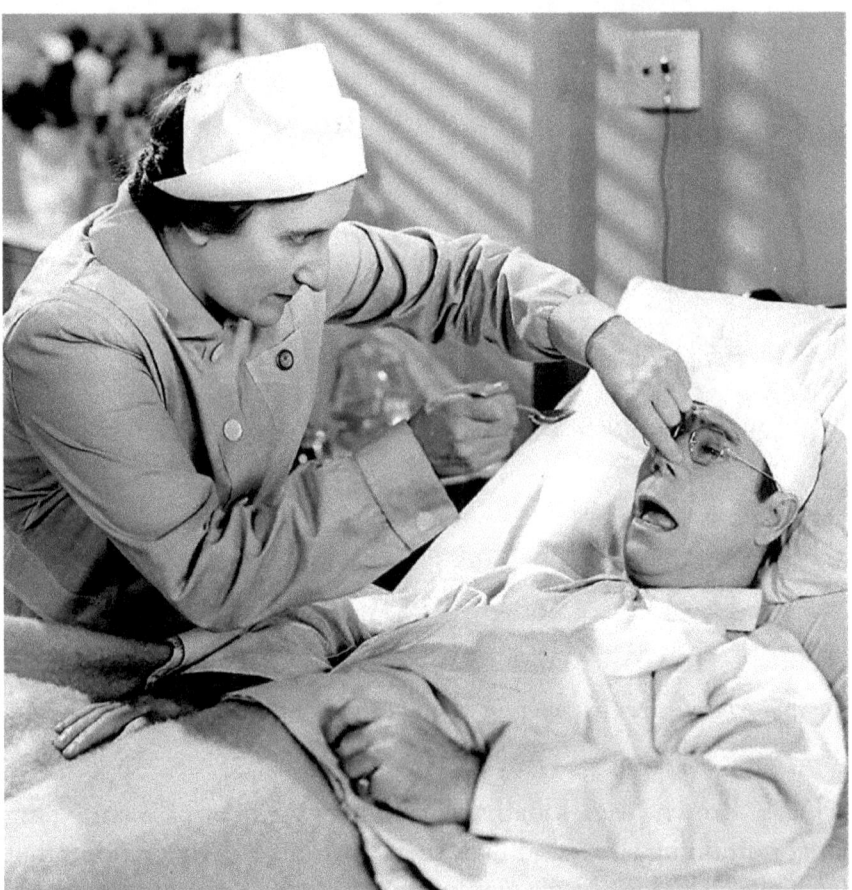

Minerva Urecal is a tough nurse for Joe in The Daring Young Man

during one of Jonathan's and Sam Long's exhibitions, Sam is hit on the head by a bowling ball, and his radio control machine is revealed. Although Jonathan was an unwitting accomplice, he is attacked by the crowd and ends up in the hospital. Ann helps him escape and he goes to the spies' hideout. Naturally the movie ends with Jonathan thwarting the spy ring in a slapstick melee.

The Daring Young Man was originally titled *Brownie*, and production was to commence in early June. The title was changed to *The Daring Young Man* in late June and at that time Marguerite Chapman was announced as the female lead. The movie was in production for one month, from June 24 until July 24, 1942, during which Joe's previous film, *Joan of Ozark*, went into release.

The Daring Young Man is very much like all of Joe E. Brown's comedies made for his Columbia contract – pleasant, disarming, unremarkable, and silly, with a good dose of slapstick. By this time, Joe E. Brown was considered a low rent comic in B movies, so his films were popular at that level. *The Daring Young Man* was well received by moviegoers, as it was often paired with a popular western at neighborhood theaters. Only in some instances did the movie play in support of a major studio feature at the better theaters.

And as with most of Joe's Columbia output, there are several amusing highlights in *The Daring Young Man*. First, his role as his character's own Grandmother allows him to play off of himself with two different characters as he had in *So You Won't Talk*. Grandma's exploits are tangential to the immediate narrative, but funny just the same. When Jonathan's business fails and Grandma must find a place to live, she ends up in a retirement home where her gambling prowess results in her winning the building from its owner, allowing her to take over. One of the more amusing scenes in the film is her presiding over the board behind a desk, and proclaiming "no bedtime, dances every night," and other such luxuries; presiding over the other elderly residents. Again, Brown does a great job crafting two distinct characters in the same movie.

The bowling scenes are essentially reliant on mechanical gags, but Joe responds well. At first, Jonathan is so inept he doesn't release his fingers from the bowling ball and slides down the alley. When he finally does release, the ball slides down the gutter, then pops out and bowls a strike. It sometimes bounces over to another alley and knocks those pins down. There is even a scene where the ball only knocks down nine pins, then comes back to hit the last one. Despite this being a B movie, Columbia had to have a bowling alley set built for the movie because the actual bowling alleys in the area were constantly crowded with defense workers.

The Nazi spies, played by Claire Dodd, Lloyd Bridges, and Donald Douglas, are the villains but also presented as ridiculous as per the usual presentation of "the enemy" in wartime comedies. At one point, Bridges' character describes something positive as being "kosher," and gets an angry reprimand from the others. The slapstick finale, when they are subdued by Jonathan, includes being blinded by makeup powder, squirted with water, and slipping on a bathroom floor that Jonathan covers with soap. The FBI arrives with the fire department, and Jonathan lures the two men to the window and flips them out where they fall onto the net and are captured. He struggles with the woman on the ledge until she too falls. And then so does Jonathan, but he bounces back up trampoline-style.

Critics were generally accepting of the film, but didn't consider it anything truly worth noting. *The Motion Picture Herald* stated:

> Admirers of that hapless young man Joe E. Brown may follow him through this fruitless tour of the service enlistment centers, a brief reign as a bowling champion, and a recurrent but never serious spy plot in this latest comedy. They will recognize several of his old gags in a new guise, as well as some novel situations with familiar twists. And the result should meet with their expectations.[72]

Audiences were satisfied with *The Daring Young Man* just as they were by the films in the Blondie series made by the same team. The two screenwriters would continue to enjoy success until their left wing politics resulted in their being blacklisted in the 1950s, ending each woman's career. As a group, the Columbia features that Joe E. Brown starred in were uniformly better than the indie efforts he did for David Loew, save for *The Gladiator*, which was perhaps his best film since leaving Warner Brothers.

The Daring Young Man was released on October 8, 1942. At that time Joe E. Brown was appearing in *The Show Off* on stage, and took a turn behind the ticket counter at the box office, much to the delight of his fans. He signed autographs and kibbitzed, having a good time. Joe was awaiting a phone call from his eldest son Don, who was a Captain in the army air corps. When a call from the Air Transport Command came through, Joe delightedly answered it, only to be told that Don was killed in a plane crash during a routine flight. Joe would later recall that his world ended at that moment. Don and some others from his troop had recently come to see Joe perform in *The Show Off,* and visited backstage afterward. They

---

72 The Daring Young Man review. *Motion Picture Herald*. December 19, 1942

even helped out with a war bond drive the comedian was hosting. Joe set up a Pacific tour to begin upon his completing filming his next movie, which was already scheduled. He planned to dedicate this tour to the memory of Don.

Don's death is part of the reason why Joe E. Brown decelerated his movie activities hereafter. He was no longer in demand as a star comic, was co-starring in films at a low budget studio, and he felt a need to tour the army bases during the war. But he was committed to finish the films he agreed to do for Republic Pictures, the next of which was *Chatterbox*, which once again paired him with Judy Canova.

CHATTERBOX

Directed by Joseph Santley
Screenplay: George Carleton Brown and Frank Gill Jr.
Produced by Albert J. Cohen
Cinematography: Ernest Miller
Film Editing: Ernest J. Nims.

Songs
Why Can't I Sing a Love Song?
Written by Harry Akst and Sol Meyer

Welcome to Victory Ranch
Written by Harry Akst and Sol Meyer

Sweet Lucy Brown
Written by Leon René and Otis René

Mad About Him, Sad Without Him, How Can I Be Glad Without Him Blues
Written by Larry Markes and Dick Charles

Cast:
Joe E. Brown, Judy Canova, Rosemary Lane, John Hubbard, Gus Schilling, Chester Clute, Anne Jeffreys, Emmett Vogan, George Byron, Billy Bletcher, Spade Cooley, The Mills Brothers, Marie Windsor, Dorothy Andre, Judy Clark, Maxine Doyle, Mary Kenyon, Pat Starling, Jane Weeks, Mary Armstrong, Gary Bruce, Nora Lane, Robert Conway, Mike Lally, Gordon DeMain, Matty Kemp, Dickie Dillon, Buzz Henry, Earle Hodgins, Pedro DePaul, Edward Earle, Sam Flint, Tex Williams, Pierce Lyden, Art Whitney, Ben Taggart, Pat McKee, Charles Williams, Frank Melton, Tom Quinn, Ray Parsons, George Magrill, Joe Phillips, Bill and Joe Yrigoyen, Ruth Robinson.

Released April 27, 1943
Running time: 77 minutes

Republic Pictures
Black and White

In his second teaming with Judy Canova, Joe E. Brown has a much bigger role and the story is about him. This is closer to a Joe E. Brown movie, but the film's purpose is still an effort to spotlight Republic Pictures star Canova, even though Joe's character is as central to the narrative.

Joe E. Brown plays Rex Vane, a popular cowboy star on a radio show. B.O., the head of Mammoth Pictures, wants to make a cowboy star out of Rex, believing the popularity of his radio show could translate to the movie box office. The problem is, Rex is, in reality a city bred actor who has never been west of Chicago, and has never ridden a horse. Rex, however, believes that he can still do the movies, because he is an actor who has studied "all of Roy Rogers' pictures." When he and his manager Roger Grant (Emmett Vogan) arrive at a Dude Ranch, columnist Carol Forrest (Rosemary Lane) asks Rex to get on a horse for a photo. Rex, wanting to keep up the ruse that he is an actual cowboy, agrees, but the horse is spooked by the nearby yodeling of Judy Boggs (Judy Canova). Rex is thrown from the horse and nearly trampled, but Judy saves him. The publicity from this event causes Rex to be exposed as a phony and his radio show is cancelled. However, B.O. still wants to make the movie, but with Judy as Rex's co-star. Rex tries to restore his popularity by setting up a scene where he rescues Judy. She agrees to this, feeling badly that she was indirectly involved in exposing Rex and he has told her that his mother may have to be sent to the poorhouse. When they try to shoot the scene, Rex's insistence on performing his own stunts, and Judy's terrible acting, upset the director, Sebastian Smart (John Hubbard) and writer George Gillie (Gus Schilling). They decide to save the project by making it into a comedy. Meanwhile, Judy discovers that Rex has no mother, so to prove himself, Rex dons a disguise and pretends to be his own mother. Later, when doing a scene where Judy is in a cabin set for demolition and rescued by Rex in the nick of time, the two end up trapped in the cabin when an actual explosion takes place, and in

Ad for Chatterbox

the melee, Rex actually does save Judy's life. This restores his career, and the two are married.

At least as funny as *Joan of Ozark*, and filled with amusing highlights, moviegoers responded quite favorably to *Chatterbox*. Critics, however, dismissed it as an unremarkable B effort. The review in the trade magazine *Film Daily* stated:

> The names of Joe E. Brown and Judy Canova should be the salvation of *Chatterbox*, a slight comedy that strives pretty hard to put over its laughs, which are not in abundance. Since the two comics possess a sizeable following, the exhibitor will not be taking any appreciable risk in playing the film. The film depends for most of its fun on two or three stock situations that have been excellently developed and milked for all they're worth. Miss Canova is given ample opportunity to sing.[73]

Despite the misgivings of the critics, exhibitors reported that the film was quite popular and drew good laughs, especially in small towns and rural areas.

Perhaps the screenwriters took a peek at the wildly popular Abbott and Costello features being produced by Universal studios. Their 1942 film *Ride Em Cowboy* features Dick Foran as a popular western novelist who does a personal appearance at a dude ranch, and must hide the fact that he has none of the skills as he states in his books. Abbott and Costello were enjoying the sort of top-level box office popularity that Joe E. Brown achieved ten years earlier, so it would stand to reason that some of the ideas in their comedies could inspire screenwriters at the smaller studios. Also, the inclusion of The Mills Brothers mirrors Bud and Lou featuring The Ink Spots in their pictures. Also, it's just as likely that they took inspiration from other films from Republic Pictures, seeing as how their most popular films at the time were westerns. In some ways this movie feels like a parody of those.

It is impressive that Joe E. Brown performs with the same enthusiasm as any of his previous pictures in that it is his first since the tragedy with his son. However, while the teaming of Canova and

---

73 Chatterbox review. *Film Daily*. April 12, 1943

Brown was really catching on with audiences, and the two enjoyed working together, Joe backed out of the scheduled next project with Judy. He was set to co-star with her in *Sleepy Lagoon*, scheduled to be shot after production completed on *Chatterbox*, but Joe wanted to get away from the studio and return to live performances at army bases. This activity was more beneficial in his coping with the grief of losing his son.

Upon the completion of production on *Chatterbox* in January of 1942, Joe E. Brown went on a three-month tour performing in a variety of different shows for the military. According to Wes Gehring's book *Joe E. Brown: Film Comedian and Baseball Buffoon*:

> So, what constituted a show for the comedian? While there was never a set program (Brown liked to improvise) one can piece together a good idea from period articles and Joe's World War 2 memoir *Your Kids and Mine*. The show would begin with a group singing of "God Bless America." Then, following a tradition that dated back at least to his 1936 London Palladium performance, he would construct a comedy collage, both discussing and drawing from his films. Given that the comedian loved baseball and felt that his best movies were the diamond trilogy of *Fireman Save My Child*, *Elmer The Great*, and *Alibi Ike*, it should come as no surprise that a major source of his live comedy was baseball related. Of all this diamond material, an especially popular Brown sketch on his military tour was to pantomime the Elmer pitching routine, including a comic corkscrew windup.[74]

Joe E. Brown returned to the states in the Spring of 1943, as he still owed Republic Pictures one more movie. He planned to return to live performances for the troops in November of that year, but he had time to not only film *Casanova in Burlesque* for Republic, he also re-teamed with Martha Raye for a supporting role in a big budget color movie at 20th Century Fox featuring Betty Grable.

---

74 Gehring, Wes. *Joe E. Brown: Film Comedian and Baseball Buffoon*. Jefferson, NC: McFarland, 2006

CASANOVA IN BURLESQUE

Directed by Leslie Goodwins
Screenplay: Frank Gill Jr. from a story by John Wales
Produced by Albert J. Cohen
Cinematography: Reggie Lanning
Film Editing: Ernest J. Nims.

Songs
Casanova Joe
Music by Walter Kent
Lyrics by Kim Gannon

Who Took Me Home Last Night?
Music by Jule Styne
Lyrics by Harold Adamson

Five-A-Day Fatima
Music by Walter Kent
Lyrics by Kim Gannon

Willie the Shake
Music by Walter Kent
Lyrics by Kim Gannon

Mess Me Up
Music by Walter Kent
Lyrics by Kim Gannon

Taming of the Shrew Routine
Music by Walter Kent
Lyrics by Kim Gannon

Cast:
Joe E. Brown, June Havoc, Dale Evans, Marjorie Gateson, Lucien Littlefield, Ian Keith, Roger Imhof, Harry Tyler, Patricia Knox, Sugar Geise, Jerry Frank, Margia Dean, William Benge, Howard

Hickman, Muray Parker, Jack Rice, Tudor Williams, Buster Brodie, Hariette Haddon, Kendall Bryson, Madeline Gray, Lucille Byron, Sam Flint, Joe Cappo, Helen Dickson, Sam Finn, James Carlisle, Gertrude Farnum, Dean Collins, Lew Davis, Edythe Elliot, Dorothy Stevens, Rosemonde James, Phyllis Herrin, Maurice St Clair, Marian Kerrigan, Beverly Reedy, Isabel LaMal, Patti Posten, Rose Morel, Murray Parker.

Released April 27, 1943
Running time: 77 minutes
Republic Pictures
Black and White

To finish off his contract agreement with Republic Pictures, Joe E. Brown was cast in a movie that pleased him greatly immediately upon reading the script. As far back as his Warner Brothers days, Joe wanted to expand his horizons as an actor. An attempt to do so with *A Very Honorable Guy* resulted in a good movie that audiences weren't ready to accept. However, by this point in his career, when Joe no longer had to maintain top level box office and was decelerating his activities in movies, he was in a perfect position to stretch, and play a more serious, layered role. The fact that *Casanova in Burlesque* also offered Joe the opportunity to perform some of his Burlesque material made it, in his eyes, the perfect project.

Joe E. Brown plays Joseph Kelly, a college professor who teaches Shakespeare classes and is considered one of the finest educators and authorities on the Bard in the University system. During the summer break when colleges are not in session, Joseph performs in a Burlesque show. He keeps each activity quiet from the other. One of the girlie acts in the show, Lillian Coleman (June Havoc), not only discovers Joseph's status as a Professor, he arrives to find out that he has been asked to direct a Shakespearean play with amateur talent. She blackmails Joseph into casting her in the lead. However, Lillian is a bad actress. He confides in Barbara Compton (Dale Evans) daughter of the college's chief patron, Lucille Compton (Marjorie Gateson) as to why he has to keep Lillian in the cast. It is ultimately decided to hire Joseph's Burlesque cronies to put on the show, a swinging version of *Taming of the Shrew*.

June Havoc and Joe in Casanova in Burlesque

Aside from Joe E. Brown playing a serious part that is dotted with comedy, rather than a straight comedy role, it is interesting that this concept pre-dates an actual musical version of *Taming of the Shrew*, the big budget MGM production *Kiss Me Kate*, which came out nearly a decade later. Despite this being a low budget Republic Picture, *Casanova in Burlesque* comes off as an amusing, clever movie and Joe E. Brown does a great job in an offbeat role.

Joe playing a straight part, and so effectively, was something of a portent. It presented his ability as an actor beyond his noted comedy, and in a few years when television offered more consistent and lucrative opportunities, he was able to play both comedy and drama. But this is not to say that Brown maintained a serious demeanor throughout the proceedings. He still finds himself in embarrassing situations where he has to stammer out an excuse and gets drunk with a Barrymoresque Shakespearean actor.

Joe and June Havoc play Shakespeare in Casanova in Burlesque

The opening and conclusion of the film allows a bit of a tour de force for Brown. He opens with a couple of Burlesque skits in which he gets to do dialect humor, eccentric dancing, and slapstick. And, though now past 50, Joe E. Brown can still execute a perfect backflip as he had years earlier in the theatrical comedy *Bright Lights*. The concluding scene where the Burlesque performers swing through Shakespeare is the movie's highlight. Twisting the Bard's words with jive, adding upbeat songs, the rousing comical method is a hit with the audience and the moral appears to be that the haughty legitimate theater and the lower-class Burlesque houses have more in common than a pretentious person may care to admit. The Burlesque sequences give Brown plenty of opportunity to inject some more comedy into his performance, and the scenes that hark back to his vaudeville origins, are great.

June Havoc was always good when playing a gum-snapping, wise-cracking lady in the traditional sense of 1940s cinema, and it is fun to see a cute, pert Dale Evans playing a role away from hubby Roy Rogers and his westerns for the same studio. Lucien Littlefield, who had worked with Joe memorably in *The Gladiator* and also in *Wide Open Faces*, makes a welcome appearance in this movie, and character actor Jack Rice is quite amusing as a harried, fluttery costume designer.

Exhibitors, for the most part, hailed *Casanova in Burlesque* as a fun musical comedy while some stated their audiences were disappointed that it was so atypical of Joe E. Brown. However, Joe himself was pleased with the role, satisfied with his performance, and enjoyed the experience. But he was wanting to get back out on the road to perform more stage shows for the troops.

Marjorie Gateson, Joe E. Brown, and Jack Rice in Casanova in Burlesque

Before he would undertake his next tour, however, Joe agreed to re-team with Martha Raye at 20th Century Fox for his first A-level picture for a top studio in nearly ten years. *Pin Up Girl* was lavish color musical starring Betty Grable, who had become the army's pin up, her poster becoming a big hit among servicemen. The publicity surrounding Joe being hired to appear in a film with Betty Grable, caused the army to name him their "pin-up boy," a gag that delighted the comedian. Once again being in a top-level movie for a major studio buoyed Joe's spirits, even if it was in a supporting role. And after he finished work on *Pin Up Girl*, he could return to entertaining his beloved troops. In an interview at the time, Joe said he hoped to make it to the fighting men in Italy on his next tour.

PIN UP GIRL

Directed by H. Bruce Humberstone
Screenplay: Robert Ellis, Helen Logan, Earl Baldwin from a story by Libbie Block
Produced by William LeBaron
Cinematography: Ernest Palmer
Film Editing: Robert Simpson

Songs
You're My Little Pin Up Girl
Music by James V. Monaco
Lyrics by Mack Gordon

Time Alone Will Tell
Music by James V. Monaco
Lyrics by Mack Gordon

Red Robins, Bobwhites and Bluebirds
Music by James V. Monaco
Lyrics by Mack Gordon

Don't Carry Tales out of School
Music by James V. Monaco
Lyrics by Mack Gordon

Yankee Doodle Hayride
Music by James V. Monaco
Lyrics by Mack Gordon

Once Too Often
Music by James V. Monaco
Lyrics by Mack Gordon

The Story of the Very Merry Widow
Music by James V. Monaco
Lyrics by Max Gordon

Cast:
Betty Grable, John Harvey, Martha Raye, Joe E. Brown, Eutene Pallette, Dorthea Kent, Dave Willock, Leon Belasco, Marcel Dallo, B.S. Pully, Irving Bacon, Nat King Cole, Reed Hadley, J. Farrell MacDonald, Mantan Morland, Charles Moore, Fredie Steele, Ruth Warren, Walter Tetley, Max Willenz, Bert Moorehouse, Hermes Pan, Lillian Porter, Bonnie Bannon, Robert Homans, Jackie Barnett, Neal Hefti, Angela Blue, Eddie Hall, Roger Clark, Jesse Graves, James Conaty, Karen X. Gaylord, Bess Flowers, Skating Vanities, Nick and Steve Condos, Charlie Spivak and his Orchestra.

Released April 25, 1944
Running time: 84 minutes
20th Century Fox
Technicolor

Energetic musicals in Technicolor became something of a staple for 20th Century Fox during the war years, and *Pin Up Girl* was designed to capitalize on Betty Grable's popularity with service men. Thus, *Pin Up Girl* is a Betty Grable musical, with John Harvey as her obligatory handsome leading man. Joe E Brown stars as a nightclub owner and Martha Raye as his star attraction, a comedy musical performer who headlines at his club. *Pin Up Girl* is a delightful example of a musical comedy from this period, with a light narrative, bright Technicolor, fun songs, and amusing novelty numbers. Perhaps it can be argued that it doesn't belong in an assessment of Joe E. Brown's filmography, as he only offers support in someone else's movie. But It is an important film in Joe's career. It shows his transition to character roles, which he used to balance out his career in the 1950s, and shows him in a straight part that relies little on his established comic skills.

This project was originally announced by the studio a couple of years earlier, and to star Linda Darnell and Don Ameche. When it was decided to transform the movie into a musical and feature Betty Grable, it came at a time when Betty was seven months pregnant. It features her as Lorry, a stenographer who passes herself off as a Broadway musical star. She ends up connected with a sailor

Joe reteamed with Martha Raye in the big budget color Fox musical Pin Up Girl

(John Harvey) who uses his friendship with a night club owner (Joe E. Brown) to get Lorry a break. Ending up stuck in Washington DC, Lorry dons glasses and gets a job as the Navy man's stenographer (and he somehow doesn't recognize her merely with glasses on – shades of Clark Kent).

The film has the usual romantic situations and misconceptions in a comic manner, and while its narrative is trite and unrealistic, it is buoyed by the performances of a great cast, good humor and fun music. While he is merely a supporting role that could have been handled by any competent contract actor on the 20th Century Fox lot, Joe E. Brown was freelancing at the time, was pleased to pick up a small role in a major picture, and realized he could finish his scenes fairly quickly and start a new tour of army bases. The studio realized his name still meant something at the box office, and adding it to the cast would only assist the box office receipts.

Joe E. Brown's performance is not a comical one. It is not there to generate laughs. But in the straight role as a nightclub owner, he holds his own nicely, and comes off as secure in the role and believable. Always an actor who always liked to explore beyond the parameters of his established comic character, Joe E. Brown was pleased with this opportunity and proud of his contribution to the movie.

The dynamic between Joe and Martha Raye is good. She is very brash and comes on quite strong, and his character is more mild-mannered, so that dynamic is amusing whenever they share scenes together. There chemistry comes off so much better in this movie than in *$1000 a Touchdown*, even though they were playing leads in the latter. For instance, there is a scene that opens with Brown laying on the floor, with Martha Raye standing over him. It's clear that she knocked him out after he delivered some not great news to her, even though we never see that fight happen. And, even though Joe E. Brown is still clearly in support, his character is important to the story.

Pin Up Girl is also significant as Joe E. Brown's last movie until after the war, save for being among many brief star cameos at his old studio Warner Brothers in *Hollywood Canteen* (1944). Joe went back out on tour to entertain the troops on behalf of his late son's memory. However, he almost lost another child when his daughter, Mary Elizabeth, was involved in a serious car accident. The emergency room was overwhelmed and there was no doctor available to care for his daughter, so Joe ran through the hospital frantically trying to find an available doctor. He finally found one about to go home, and although exhausted, he recognized Joe E. Brown and agreed to treat his daughter. The result was an emergency operation that took seven hours, but saved her life. Joe then asked the doctor if he was a fan. The doctor stated that fifteen years earlier, he asked Hollywood celebrities to come to Children's Orthopedic Hospital on Christmas Eve and cheer up the youngsters who were patients. The doctor recalled that only two celebs showed up: dancer Bill Robinson, and Joe.

At the end of 1944, he released a book on his entertaining the troops, *Your Kids and Mine*. A syndicated review stated:

> Joe E. Brown, the comedian, who has visited practically every battle front in this war in his role as an entertainer, has written a book about his experiences, *Your Kids and Mine*, in which he expresses his deep pride in the moral calibre and fighting courage of the American service man. And American readers, already convinced of the truth of his testimony, but never tiring of hearing new tributes, will find occasion to be proud of an exceedingly humble and sincere individual the author himself. Before his son, Don, a captain in the Air Transport Command, had been killed in a routine flight in California, Joe E. Brown had begun his career as a war-zone trouper in the Alaskan outposts. It had been a rewarding and exhilarating even a dangerous experience, and he was resolved to go to the South Pacific front, if he could get official permission. Then this blow came and for a time Brown was in a dark abyss, but soon he remembered a remark he had made to Don during their last conversation. He had said that he might meet him in the Pacific. Well, he would not see Don, except in spirit, but he would meet thousands of other Dons. In a way he had an appointment to keep with them, because "when you have lost your own boy all other lads become your sons. And so, he went to the South Pacific. And so, he forced his "big mouth" into a smile, and told jokes, and laughed at himself; and was always ready, no matter how tired he was, or how great the technical difficulties, to give another show. He did not rate himself a great comedian he was far too modest for that but the "boys" seemed to like him, and their thundering applause warmed his heart and stimulated his imagination. In his book, he has tried to tell us about the conditions under which American soldiers lived and fought on the sectors he visited including the Aleutians, New Guinea, China and Italy. He traveled a total of 150,000 miles and at every stop he made friends not only with officers, but with the G. I's, and principally

the G. I.'s. He had a long talk with General MacArthur and wangled out of him a permit to go on a bombing mission, but the best he could achieve in the South Pacific area was a trip on a reconnaissance plane. But later in China, he was allowed to go on not one but five such missions, and he felt that even though he was a civilian and had no part in the actual bombings, he had in some way though vicariously represented Don, who all through his training had looked forward to getting at the (the enemy). Comedy and tragedy are intermingled in Joe E. Brown's account of his travels. Many ludicrous things happened and the author makes the most of these in the dozens of funny stories he tells, yet the major theme is sadness, as it must be in any reporting of war. Mr. Brown never missed a hospital, if he could help it, in any of the sectors visited, and never neglected an opportunity to seek out the badly x wounded and to carry them some message of good cheer and courage. In fact, he himself, was the pupil, as he so often says, in the matter of bravery, because in these hospitals, he learned first-hand of what fine mettle our Americans are made. Some of them were blinded, some had lost arms or legs, some of them were hopeless cases, but few of them were in despair. These men who had such grave injuries but who despite the odds, longed to recover so that they could fight again, were among Mr Brown's best audiences. From the South Pacific, Mr Brown came home for a short interval, but he was soon off again this time "from Miami to South America, across from Natal to the Gold Coast, proceeding from Nigeria to Khartoum, on through India to China, back to Burma and through Calcutta and Teheran to Cairo; then along the African coast to Algiers and across the Mediterranean to Italy." Sometimes there were generals in his audiences and once two kings attended one of his performances. A few days after the Teheran conference, he slept in the bed occupied by President Roosevelt. He came home with a feeling of great debt to the men he had entertained they had given him so much in return for the little he had been able to do for them. He, Joe E. Brown, would never cease to be grateful for this experience because it had made him a better American, broadened his horizon, enriched his understanding, strengthened his faith in his Creator. The ending of the book is skillfully managed. When he returned home he found a large number of invitations from parents who wanted him to visit them because their sons had been so appreciative of his "entertainments" out there at the front. He told his wife that it would take a couple of years to make the rounds if he were to accept those invitations, but he thought it might be possible to visit one or two of them. To his surprise his wife agreed and she looked thoughtful as she said: "Heres a man who has four sons, all of them in the service. He'd like some word about his boys. He wants you to come to dinner on the eighteenth. At his house." He was in Washington at the time, and on the eighteenth, he put the invitation card in his pocket. "Where do you want to go, sir? the taxi driver queried. But there were other riders in the machine, and Joe E. Brown, was too bashful to say the, address right out. Instead he handed the card to the driver. "Gosh," he said. "Why, that there is an invitation to the White House. Yes sir!"[75]

In 1945, Joe became one of only two civilians to receive the Bronze Star.

It was not until 1948 before Joe E. Brown appeared in another movie. Now in his middle 50s and long past his comedy movie heyday, Joe chose a film that had family appeal which he felt was perfect for the post-war era.

---

75 Swan, Addie May. Inspiring Men On Men at Front by Joe E. Brown. *The Daily Times*. December 16, 1944

THE TENDER YEARS

Directed by Harold Schuster
Screenplay: Arnold Belgard and Jack Jungmeyer from a story by Jungmeyer adapted by Abem Finkel
Produced by Edward Alperson
Cinematography: Henry Freulich
Film Editing: Richard Farrell

Cast:
Joe E. Brown, Richard Lyon, Noreen Nash, Charles Drake, Josephine Hutchinson, James Millican, Griff Barnett, Jeanne Gail, Harry Chesire, Blayney Lewis, Jimmie Dodd, Joyce Arling, Charles McQuarry, Lane Chandler, Kate Mackenna, Hank Patterson, Stanley Blystone, Edmund Cobb, Marjorie Eaton, Milton Kibbee, Charles Jordan, Maynard Holmes, Ben Erway, Gene Collins.

Released January 3, 1948
Running time: 71 minutes
Alson Productions for 20th Century Fox
Black and White

After the war ended, Joe E. Brown toured in the play *Harvey*, best known for the film version starring James Stewart. Brown was a big hit in the role, his performances were well-reviewed and well-received. In his personal life, Joe renewed his vows with his wife in 1947; they had married in 1915. But Joe E. Brown had not appeared in a movie since 1944, other than the fact that David Loew re-released several of his Joe E. Brown productions in 1945.

The Tender Years was Joe's first new movie in several years, and it is not a comedy at all. It is a serious drama in which Joe plays Will Norris, pastor of a small town church in the 1880s. A newcomer to town, Kit Barton (James Millican), is running a dog fighting ring,

In his last starring film, Joe plays it straight as a country preacher in The Tender Years

and whenever one of his dogs loses a fight, he beats it bloody. This happens to his dog Slasher, so the dog runs away and seeks refuge at Pastor Norris' farm. When the dog is discovered by the Pastor's son Ted (Richard Lyon), the animal is frightened at first but is eventually tamed and made into a friendly family pet. When Kit Barton claims the dog, his intentions and actions are discovered, and Ted does not want to return him. This puts the pastor in a dilemma, for he realizes that Kit is the rightful owner, but it goes against his nature as a clergyman to "steal" the dog, despite its abusive owner.

The Tender Years is an independent production, produced by Edward Alperson who had once headed Grand National Pictures. He was now producing low budget films to be released through 20th Century Fox, and was able to get Joe E. Brown's services for only $20,000. Brown was pleased to not only have a serious dramatic role that was perfect for his talents, it was also something to which he could relate. Growing up in the circus and seeing a lot of animals mistreated, Brown was very interested in playing a man who takes a stand in order to save one. The film had good bookings in neighborhood theaters, and since Joe had been away from movies for years, audiences were not expecting him to play in a comedy. The children who had loved his comic roles in the 30s were now young adults, many of them parents, and they were pleased to see an older Joe E. Brown in an emotional and uplifting family drama.

Joe E. Brown also received great critical notices for taking on a serious role. Brown had long ago proven himself as a good actor, and maintained his skills in stage productions, so there was nothing rusty about his performance. It is seasoned, measured, and actually quite brilliant. The film was endorsed by the humane society and other animal welfare organizations, which further helped its box office appeal.

While there are comic highlights in Joe E. Brown's older movies, in this one there are impressive emotional scenes. When Ted and his young friend Jeanie first go to return the dog, which has been named Dusty, they discover Kit whipping dogs into a frenzy, forcing them to fight each other. When Kit comes to the Norris home and takes a barking, yelping Dusty with him, the pastor stands by powerless, desperately offering to buy the dog. Kit tells him that the dog will make him $500 in one fight, even if he loses. And the emotional scenes between father and son, remind us how well Joe always related to children. Even during the post-war years, when editorials blamed a juvenile delinquency problem on everything from comic books to rock and roll, Joe always defended the youth. Just as he remained supportive of animal welfare.

What is so impressive about Joe's character is the way he reconciles breaking the law to help save the dog. The reverend helps his son steal Dusty back after Kit takes him away, but then turns himself in, and until the end of the movie is prepared to stand trial for theft. He goes through a lot of growth in the way he views Dusty. At the beginning of the film, he refers to the dogs as "dumb animals," but by the end he recognizes that all living creatures deserve to be treated with kindness. *The Tender Years* is one of the earliest ones to portray dog-fighting in such a way and really advocate against the inhumanity of the sport.

Edwin Schallert, film critic for *The Los Angeles Times* was suitably impressed by the production and by Joe E. Brown's performance:

> *The Tender Years* is a surprisingly good film in purposefulness. Actually, it has less to do with the work of a churchman along formal lines than it probably should have, but the central figure's missionary work in behalf of the humane treatment of animals contains large audience appeal. There is also in this cinema a return to the fine simplicity of the rural narrative that reflects on an earlier, gentler period of American life. Its story about the saving of a dog from a cruel master, who specializes in staging pit fights between canines, is sensitively told, and incidentally exploits the devotion between Brown as a father and his son who is well enacted by young Richard Lyon. Brown deserves plaudits for the reserve of his performance in an unusual role, as remote from his former comedy exuberances as might be imagined. It is he and Lyon who share the major duties. There is much sympathetic charm in this moving little story.[76]

---

76 Schallert, Edwin. Tender Years Genuinely Appealing. *The Los Angeles Times*. January 31, 1948

While the trade periodical *Film Daily* was also suitably impressed by both the movie and Joe's performance:

> Smart know how in production and keen understanding of what will capture the attention of the audience insofar as the story values are involved, lifts *The Tender Years* at once into the sphere of better grade product. What the audience will expect in this appearance of Joe E. Brown, after a long absence, is one thing. They'll get no raucous comedy. He acquits himself of a fine human performance repleate with dignity and good taste. He does it with such skill that he will stop the spectator cold. As he builds his role he creates a warmth that will make itself immediately felt.[77]

The Tender Years was Joe E. Brown's last leading role in a theatrical film. For the remainder of his active career, he would concentrate more on the new medium of television and the stage. He would also take on supporting roles in major theatrical films, including the movie that continues to define his career.

However, the fact that *The Tender Years* concludes Joe E. Brown's work as a movie leading man is still significant, just as *The Daring Young Man* had been the last of his solo starring comedy vehicles. It culminates a long career of comedy features, by a man who spent several years among the very top box office stars in movies.

---

77 Tender Years Review. *Film Daily*. December 3, 1947.

SOME LIKE IT HOT AND THE LATER YEARS

As the 1940s became the 1950s, Joe E. Brown explored the new medium of television, appearing on both comedy-variety programs like *The Ed Wynn Show* as well as exploring his acting ability in dramatic anthologies. He even guested on the game show *Name's The Same*, running the gamut of what was popular on the small screen during its early years. Joe was now long past his top stardom as a movie comedian, but his name still meant something to television viewers and moviegoers. The children who grew up with Joe's comedies in the 1930s were now parents of households who were buying TVs and watching television shows with their families. They were happy to see old favorite Joe in comic and dramatic performances, along with introducing their children to his old movies when telecast.

We can recall Joe's longing to stretch beyond the parameters of his established screen persona way back in the Warner years, and understand what a gratifying experience it was to explore various aspects of his talent during his later years. Television needed content, and at frist many of the major studios saw it as competition and wouldn't allow their films to be telecast. So, to have notable film actors like Joe E. Brown available for both comic and dramatic roles was something of a coup for early TV producers.

This is not to say that Joe E. Brown eschewed motion picture work at this time. Joe's first movie of the 1950s was as Captain Andy in a lavish Technicolor remake of *Show Boat*, which had already been most notably filmed in 1936 with Charles Winninger in the role. Of course, it is up to the individual viewer as to which version is better, but the 1951 movie n which Joe appears, also stars Kathryn Grayson, Howard Keel, and Ava Gardner, and also includes the great Jerome Kern-Oscar Hammerstein II score featuring songs like "Old Man River" and "Can't Help Loving That Man."

Joe had a supporting role as Captain Andy in Show Boat *(1951)*

The Tender Years and, to some extent, *Pin Up Girl*, were each something of an apprenticeship for Joe, whose role as Captain Andy is a very anchored, secure, serious, but lovable character. It draws upon several traits Joe established in the various characters he played when he was allowed to venture beyond his comedy. Because the film was such big production, Joe's excellent portrayal did not get as much attention as it deserved, most of the publicity concentrating on the younger actors. Joe took things like this in stride. He returned to working in television productions for the next several years.

Joe E. Brown gave a remarkably good perforamce as an aging clown in *The Buick Circus Hour*, telecast once-monthly in place of the wildly popular *Milton Berle Show*. He also went back on stage, appearing in several regional productions, including revivals of *Harvey* and *Show Boat*. Then in 1953, Joe's two daughters were married in a lavish double ceremony. They each made Joe a grandpa in 1954 when they gave birth within 48 hours of each other. In 1955, his son Joe L. Brown, who shared his father's love of baseball, became general manager of the Pittsburgh Pirates, a position he held until 1976. Thus, as the 1950s continued, Joe basked in the limelight of a new medium, secured the occasional role in a major motion picture, and enjoyed a particularly happy personal life as his family expanded to include grandchildren.

One of the true highlights of Joe E. Brown's television career was *The Silent Partner* (1955), an episode of the dramatic anthology series *Screen Director's Playhouse*. Brown plays a veteran movie producer named Arthur Vail who is accepting a lifetime achievement Oscar. He recalls in his acceptance speech the great comedies he made during the silent era with a comedian named Kelsey Dutton. The Oscars are being watched on television in a bar by a disparate group of people, including Kelsey Dutton, who is played by Buster Keaton. Clips of the comedies Vail made with Dutton are shown, and the people in the bar are laughing and enjoying the antics, while Dutton himself sits sadly, observing his past triumphs that happened so long ago. He is now just a face in the crowd, and had been since the advent of talkies. Eventually, the people in the bar (one of whom is played by ZaSu Pitts) recognize him. Word gets to Vail, who reconnects with Kelsey and plans to make him a star again.

One of many great things about *The Silent Partner* is that they don't use clips from old Keaton comedies, they actually shoot new silent comedy footage with Keaton, nearing 60 at the time, performing classic routines brilliantly. There are also appearances by Jack Kruschen, Percy Helton, and Snub Pollard. And the episode was directed by George Marshall, whose career dated back to silent comedy, and who directed Laurel and Hardy, Bob Hope, and Jerry Lewis over the years. Of course, Joe E. Brown and Buster Keaton were old friends whose baseball teams would frequently play each other as both were equally athletic.

It was 1956 before Joe E. Brown appeared in another picture, but it was another major production. Joe was one of many celebrities

Joe was one of many familiar names in Mike Todd's epic Around The World in 80 Days *(1956), which won Best Picture at the Oscars*

who had a small part in Mike Todd's epic production of Jules Verne's *Around The World in Eighty Days*. While his part was small, the film did win Best Picture at the Academy Awards, allowing Joe to have the prestige of appearing in an Oscar winner. The year 1956 also saw the release of Joe's autobiography, *Laughter is a Wonderful Thing*.

After more TV and stage work, Joe E. Brown closed out the 1950s by being cast in a role that seemed like just another supporting part, but became perhaps the most notable accomplishment in his long career. It seems that if anyone is aware of Joe E. Brown, it is because of Billy Wilder's 1959 movie *Some Like it Hot*. Joe's career has been defined by his performance as Osgood Fielding in this classic comedy which starred Tony Curtis and Jack Lemmon. They play a couple of jazz musicians who witness a gangland slaying and must flee from the gangsters, headed by George Raft, with cop played by Pat O'Brien always nearby. The musicians dress as women and join an all-girl band, both wanting to reveal their identity to a beautiful musician played by Marilyn Monroe. Joe E. Brown plays a rich, pampered sexagenarian who falls for Jack Lemmon in drag in a hilarious performance. Brown draws upon his milquetoast character of the past in that Osgood is a pampered millionaire. He draws even more specifically on the swaggering braggart that informed his characters in *Elmer the Great* and *Alibi Ike* in that Osgood exudes confidence. Osgood really believes Lemmon is a woman, actually finds him/her attractive, and is so confident and convincing, he almost has Lemmon go for him as well!

We learn in the scene where he first meets Jack Lemmon's character, his mother sent him to that hotel to stop him from chasing women, and he's been married seven or eight times. This aspect of the character feels very against type from the characters we are most familiar with Joe playing, but somehow it suits him perfectly. All of Brown's exchanges with Jack Lemmon are quite funny, especially their tango scene where Joe gets to show off his dancing skills for the last time. And Joe E. Brown gets to utter the movie's classic closing line.

Some Like It Hot was not only one of the most popular movies of 1959, it has lived on as a noted classic. The American Film Institute named *Some Like It Hot* the greatest American comedy movie, beating out such formidable contenders as Buster Keaton's *The General* and Charlie Chaplin's *Modern Times*.

There is a certain irony to Joe's popularity via *Some Like It Hot*. It isn't a Joe E. Brown movie, so it is not a part of his essential filmography. It was made years after his starring films had concluded, and nearly a quarter century since he was among the top box office stars in American cinema. Yet, because its overall production is so win-

Some Like it Hot *might be Joe's best known movie appearance, where he gives the classic closing line to Jack Lemmon*

ning, its entire structure is so comically sound, and its cast featuring stars like Curtis and Lemmon, and an enduring icon like Marilyn Monroe, it is the most noted and popular film in which Joe E. Brown appears. Even the Oscar winning *Around The World In Eighty Days* does not enjoy the lasting popularity of *Some Like It Hot.*

What the film does show is that Joe E. Brown was still a great comic actor long after his stardom had faded, his series of B movies had been completed, and his starring work represented another time and another era. Even surrounded by such a cast, Joe E. Brown's impact in *Some Like It Hot* has the same hilarious and beloved presence as he had during the height of his screen career. The fact that the film's closing line, from Joe, is as well or better remembered than it being one of the iconic Marilyn Monroe's best films is mighty impressive.

Joe E. Brown decelerated his activities in the 1960s, doing some TV work, and once again one of many celebrity cameos in an epic movie, this time Stanley Kramer's massive comedy production *It's a Mad, Mad, Mad, Mad World* (1963). Joe's last movie appearance was a small role in the offbeat Jacques Tourneur film *The Comedy of Terrors* (1963), which starred Vincent Price, Boris Karloff, and Peter Lorre. After one more TV appearance in 1964, Joe E. Brown

The small part Joe played in The Comedy of Terrors *ended his theatrical movie career.*

retired from acting. It was fitting that his last acting role was on the TV program *The Greatest Show on Earth* which is set in a circus. Joe E. Brown's career had come full circle. The comedian's legacy continued into the 1960s with Hanna-Barbera cartoon characters Lippy the Lion and Peter Potamus both inspired by Joe.

Joe E. Brown suffered a serious heart attack in 1968 and underwent cardiac surgery. For the next five years, the normally active Joe was slowed down considerably by health issues, including the arteriosclerosis from which he would die in 1973.

As amusing as he is in *Some Like It Hot*, Joe E. Brown has a strong legacy of comedy. The Warner Brothers releases during the first half of the 1930s placed him among the top ten box office stars for several years. Even as late as the 21st century, Joe E. Brown's best films still hold up as pleasant, disarming comedies featuring a consistently appealing performer.

BIBLIOGRAPHY

BOOKS

Belmer, Rudy. *Inside Warner Brothers.* NY: Simon and Schuster. 1985

Bergman, Andrew. *We're in the Money: Depression America and its Films.* Lanham, MD: Ivan R. Dee, 1992.

Brotheron, Jamie and Ted Okuda. *Dorothy Lee: The Life and Times of the Wheeler and Woolsey Girl.* Jefferson, NC: McFarland. 2013

Brown, Joe E. as told to Ralph Hancock. *Laugher is a Wonderful Thing.* NY: AS Barnes, 1956

Brown, Joe E. as told to Margaret Lee Runbeck. *Your Kids and Mine.* NY: Doubleday. 1944.

Chandler, Charlotte. *Nobody's Perfect: Billy Wilder, a Personal Biography.* NY: Simon and Schuster, 2002

Curtis, Tony and Mark A. Viera. *The Making of Some Like It Hot.* Hoboken, NJ: Wiley, 2009

Freedland, Michael. *The Warner Brothers.* NY: Doubleday, 1976

Gehring Wes. *Joe E. Brown: Film Comedian and Baseball Buffoon.* Jefferson, NC: McFarland, 2006

Hirschorn, Clive *The Warner Brothers Story* NY: Crown, 1979

Malone, Aubrey. *The Defiant One: A Biography of Tony Curtis.* Jefferson, NC: McFarland, 2013

Maltin, Leonard. *The Great Movie Comedians.* NY: Crown, 1978

Martin, Len D. *The Columbia Checklist.* Jefferson, NC: McFarland, 1986

McCaffrey, Donald. *The Golden Age of Sound Comedy.* NY: AS Barnes. 1973

Neibaur, James L. *The Fall of Buster Keaton.* Lanham, MD: Scarecrow Press. 2010

_____. *The James Cagney Films of the 1930s.* Lanham, MD. 2014

_____. *Movie Comedians.* Jefferson, NC: McFarland. 1986

_____. *The RKO Features.* Jefferson, NC: McFarland. 1994

Sennett, Ted. *Warner Brothers Presents.* New Rochell, NY: Arlington House. 1971

Warner, Jack. *My First Hundred Years in Hollywood.* NY: Random House, 1965

Widener, Don. *Lemmon: A Biography.* NY: Macmillan. 1975

ARTICLES AND REVIEWS

About Joe E. Brown and his Latest Film. *Brooklyn Times Union.* February 8, 1931.

Alibi Ike review. The New York Times. July 17, 1935

Around and About in Hollywood. *Los Angeles Times.* April 15, 1936

Bands, Motorboat And Tieups Promote Top Speed Picture. Exhibitors Herald-World. October 18, 1930.

Bike Racers Have Circled Globe Almost Eight Times. The Times. Sherveport, LA. November 27, 1934

The Barometer. Motion Picture News. June 2, 1931

Broadminded Review. *Pittsburgh Post-Gazette.* July 6, 1931

Brown Comedy Unit Assembles. Los Angels Times. November 3, 1936

Brown, Movie Clown Ready For Film Scene Here. Lincoln Journal Star. July 3, 1931

Brown's First Since Illness Opens Sunday. Kingsburg Recorder. January 5, 1933

Chatterbox review. Film Daily. April 12, 1943

Coney Island Used in New Comedy. *Rochester Democrat and Chronicle.* September 18, 1939

Coons, Robin. Empty Paper Bag. San Pedro News-Pilot. January 13, 1936

Daring Young Man review. Motion Picture Herald. December 19, 1942

Dominion Theater. Victoria Daily Times. June 26, 1932

Dorothy Dworak, Petite Blonde, Will Double For Dorothy Lee In Joe E. Brown's Picture At A. A. U. Lincoln Journal Star. July 2, 1931

Dramatic Scenes of Football Shown On Screen. Cincinnati Inquirer. November 23, 1930

Gala Opening Set For Sons O' Guns. *Brooklyn Times Union.* May 10, 1936

Great Guy Joe E. Brown. *Film Daily.* May 7, 1937

Irene Thirer column. New York Daily News. June 8, 1931

Joan of Ozark review. Film Daily. July 15, 1942

Joe E. Brown Chooses Third Comedy Under New Production Setup. Los Angeles Times. November 4, 1936

Joe E. Brown Comedy Due For Release. *The Los Angeles Times.* February 14, 1932

Joe E. Brown, Cowboy. *The Los Angeles Times.* February 9, 1932

Joe E Brown has Heavy Support in The Tenderfoot. Marshall Evening Chronicle June 29, 1932

Joe E. Brown has the Loudest Wardrobe in Hollywood. *San Francisco Examiner.* Sept 7, 1930 Joe E. Brown, Movie Comedian, To Use A. A. U, Games Here As Locale For His Next Screen Appearance. Lincoln Journal Star. June 26, 1931

Joe E. Brown on Twin Bill. *Santa Cruz Evening News.* July 1, 1937

Joe E. Brown Plays for Art. The San Francisco Examiner. November 20, 1935

Joe E Brown Scores Another Comedy Hit. *The San Francisco Chronicle.* November 28, 1936

Joe E. Brown's Latest Picture. Mendocino Coast Beacon. October 3, 1936

Joe Brown's New One Demands Real Acting. *New York Daily News.* May 12, 1931.

Joe E. Brown's New Picture. Democrat and Chronicle. Rochester, NY. July 26, 1931

Joe Spoils The Scene. *San Pedro News-Pilot.* July 23, 1936

Krug, Karl. Maybe It's Love review. The Pittsburgh Press. October 17, 1930

Movie Lion Lunges at Film Comedian. *Racine Journal Times.* February 16, 1934

On With The Show at Carolina Tomorrow. *Greenville News.* July 28, 1929

Parsons, Louella. Fireman Save My Child is next Joe E. Brown Talkie.

Universal Syndicate. October 7, 1931

Parsons, Louella. Joe E. Brown To Star in Musical Film. The Sacramento Bee. November 21, 1935

Plan Early Production of Joe E. Brown Film. *The Brooklyn Daily Eagle*. February 15, 1932

Sawdust to have Realism. Los Angeles Times. February 13, 1934

Scallert, Edwin. Maybe It's Love review. The Los Angeles Times. October 20, 1930.

Schallert, Edwin. Tender Years Genuinely Appealing. *The Los Angeles Times*. January 31, 1948

Scott, John. Comic Proves Versatile: Joe E. Brown Portrays Combination Fireman and Ball Player in New Film. The Los Angeles Times. February 13, 1932

Scott, John. Joe E. Brown Turns Gob. Los Angeles Times. December 29, 1933

Set New Brown Film. Motion Picture Daily. October 17, 1937

Shark Cuts Short Filming of Joe E. Brown Scene. Santa Cruz Evening News. December 26, 1932

Showman's Reviews. *Motion Picture Herald*. June 20, 1936

Shut My Big Mouth review. Photoplay. March, 1942

Soanes, Wood. Secrets of Directors Revealed. *Oakland Tribune*. August, 29, 1929

Swan, Addie May. Inspiring Men On Men at Front by Joe E. Brown. The Daily Times. December 16, 1944

Syndicated press release obtained from The San Francisco Examiner, July 2, 1935 issue

Tender Years Review. *Film Daily*. December 3, 1947

Tenderfoot review. Film Daily. May 22, 1932

Tenderfoot review. New York Daily News. May 21, 1932

Tourney Victor To Give Joe E. Brown Souvenir: Film Comedian, Owner of Largest Sport Collection, to See Final Two Days of Play. Oakland Tribune. August 31, 1939.

Tucker, George. Pictures of Manhattan. Syndicated wire service. August 27, 1942.

Two Films Await Comedian Brown. Los Angeles Times. May 19, 1934.

Ty Cobb and Babe Ruth May Take Part in Diamond Epic. The Sacramento Bee. Feb 7, 1935

Vale, Virginia. Star Dust column. Western Newspaper Union. July 17, 1940

Very Honorable Guy review. Film Daily. May 18, 1934

What The Picture Did For Me. Motion Picture Herald. March 24, 1934, April 1934, January 9, 1937

INTERNET SOURCES

Another Nice Mess. www.lordheath.com

Internet Movie Database. www.imdb.com

Mangum, John. "A Midsummer Night's Dream" (complete): Felix Mendelssohn. www.hollywoodbowl.com.

Wikipedia. www.wikipedia.org

INDEX

Abbott and Costello 122, 188, 191, 209
Abbott and Costello Meet Frankenstein 191
Africa Screams 191
All Quiet on the Western Front 62
Alperson, Edward 225
Ameche, Don 217
Animal Crackers 35
Arbuckle, Fatty 63
Around The World in Eighty Days 231, 233
Astaire, Fred 142
Autry, Gene 192, 195
Bacon, Lloyd 32, 41, 47, 48, 52
Badlanders, The 175
Baldwin, Earl 54, 88
Banks, Monty 54
Barratt, Robert 79
Barton, Charles 191
Bates, Granville 138
Beany and Cecil Show, The 141
Beaumont, Harry 138, 140
Beddoe Don 192
Bennett, Joan 17, 18, 19, 20, 21, 22
Big Broadcast of 1938 174
Blondell, Joan 1121, 122, 123
Blore, Eric 121, 175
Bogart, Humphrey 129
Bolton, Guy 6
Bond, Lillian 41
Bond, Ward 86
Bosworth, Hobart 31
Bridges, Lloyd 189, 203
Brown, Donald (Joe's son) 2, 187, 204-205
Brown, Joe L. (Joe's son) 1, 2, 181, 187, 230
Brown, Katheryn (Joe's wife) 3, 187

Brown, Kathryn (Joe's daughter) 183, 184, 230
Brown, Mary (Joe's daughter) 219, 230
Buick Circus Hour 229
Butter and Egg Man, The 54-55
Caesar, Arthur 47, 48, 54
Cagney, James 64, 76, 94, 109, 111, 114, 115, 116, 129
Caldwell, William 84
Canova, Judy 193, 194, 195, 197, 198, 199, 205, 206, 207, 209
Cantrell, Guy 100
Carle, Richard 54
Carlisle, Mary 179, 180
Carrillo, Leo 167
Ceiling Zero 129
Chapman Marguerite 201, 202
Chase, Charley 155
Circus Kid, The 2-3
Claire, Bernice 12
Clampett, Robert 141
Clark, Harry 138, 140
Clyde, Andy 59, 155
Cody, Lew 55, 58
Cohn, Harry 155, 177
Cole, Leonard "King" 100
College 44
Collier, William 36
Comedy of Terrors, The 233-234
Compson, Betty 4
Conlin, Jimmy 175
Corny Concerto 141
Coveleski, Frank 67
Cowan, Jerome 197
Cox, Dick 100
Crawford, Joan 110
Crowd Roars, The 109
Curtis, Tony 232
Daniels, Bebe 46

Dark Passage 175
Darnell, Linda 217
Darro, Frankie 2-3
Davidson, William 84
Daves, Delmer 175
Davis, Bette 129
De Cordoba, Pedro 190
De Havilland, Olivia 97, 98, 122
Del Ruth, Roy 30
Dell, Claudia 30
Demarest, William 84
Destination Tokyo 175
Dietrich, Marlene 46
Dirty Work 160, 166
Disney, Walt 192
Dodd, Claire 68, 203
Donnelly, Ruth 98
Douglas, Donald 203
Downing, Joe 160
Doyle, Maxine 89, 94
Duffy, Jack 7
Dugan, Tom 84, 185
Dumbo 192
Duna, Steffi 167
Durante, Jimmy 52
Durst, Cedric 100
Dvorak, Ann 104, 109
Dworak, Dorothy 46
Eburne, Maude 138
Ed Wynn Show, The 228
Elliot, Gordon 133
Ellis, Patricia 68, 84, 104, 109
Enright, Ray 47, 48, 54, 58
Evans, Dale 212, 215
Fairbanks, Douglas 113
Fairbanks, Douglas jr. 64
Feld, Fritz 189, 190, 192, 193
Fields, Stanley 158, 160, 168
Fields, WC 136, 160, 174
Five Marvelous Ashtons 1
Flirting With Fate 166
Footlight Parade 109
Foran, Dick 125
Ford, John 185, 192
Foster, Preston 63-64

Foy, Eddy jr. 197
Frawley, William 98
Freshman, The
G-Men 109
Gable, Clark 52
Gallagher, Skeets 133
Gargan, William 105
Gateson, Marjorie 212
Gazella, Mike 100
Gehring, Wes 52, 67, 68
General, The 232
Give Me a Sailor 174
Grable, Betty 210, 215, 216, 217
Gray, Lawrence 25
Grayson, Kathryn 228
Greatest Show on Earth, The 234
Gregory, Paul 30
Gribbon, Harry 63
Grieg, Robert 55
Griffith, Raymond 62
Hagney, Frank 32
Hall, James 18, 21
Hall, Ruth 41
Hamilton, Margaret 138
Hanaford, Poodles 84
Hanna-Barbera 234
Harvey, John 217, 218
Havoc, June 212, 214-215
Hayward, Susan 175
Helton, Percy 230
Her Majesty Love 6
Herbert, Holmes 36
Here Comes The Navy 76
Hicks, Russell 152
Hill, Al 160
Hold 'Em Jail 20
Hold Everything 10
Holloway, Sterling 69
Holt, Tim 192
Hood, Wally 100
Hopalong Cassidy 192
Hope, Bob 174, 188, 230
Horse Feathers 20
Hoskins, Allen Clayton "Farina" 60, 61, 62, 63, 64

How Green Was My Valley 192
Howard, Olin 125
Hubbard, John 207
Hughes, Carol 125, 129, 133, 135
Hurst, Don 100
I Love Lucy 98
Ink Spots 209
Jeffreys, Anne 197
Jolley, Smead 100
Jolson, Al 119
Jory, Victor 189, 191, 192
Judels, Charles 16
Kalmar, Bert 35, 37, 39, 81, 94
Kane, Eddie 166
Karloff, Boris 41, 234
Karns, Roscoe 98
Kaufman, George S. 54
Keaton, Buster 44, 52, 100, 155, 230, 232
Keel, Howard 228
Kelly, Patsy 160
Kennedy, Edgar 59, 138
Kennedy, Tom 33
Kent, Robert 164
Kern, Jerome 6
Keystone Cops 63
Kibbee, Guy 47, 48, 52, 124, 126 129
Kibbee, Milton 103, 119, 161, 223
King Kong 141
Kolb, Clarence 179-180
Koupal, Lou 100
Kruschen, Jack 230
Lahr, Bert 10, 28
Lake, Arthur 4
Lane, Charles 153
Lane, Rosemary 207
Langdon, Harry 2, 155
Lardner, Ring 100
Last Wagon, The 175
Laurel and Hardy 52, 58, 59, 136, 160, 230
Lawrence, Marc 179, 180
Lee, Dorothy 41, 42, 44, 46
Lee, Laura 12, 14, 20, 21, 26
Lemmon, Jack 232-233
LeRoy, Mervyn 41, 45, 58, 69
Levee, Mike 110, 117
Lewis, Jerry 230
Lightner, Winnie 30-32
Little Caesar 160
Littlefield, Lucien 158. 159. 161. 163. 166. 215
Lloyd, Harold 44
Lockhart, Gene 129
Loew, David 117, 122, 136, 137, 138, 139, 140, 141, 143, 145, 150, 151, 153, 154, 155, 156, 157, 158, 161, 162, 163, 166, 167, 168, 171, 172, 177, 180, 181, 186, 204, 223
Lord, Robert 47, 48
Lorre, Peter 233
Lottery Bride, The 23
Lugosi, Bela 34-36, 38, 39
Lupien, Luppee 122
Lyon, Richard 225
Macauley, Richard 138, 145
MacDonald, Jeanette 23
MacEwan, Walter 96
Magnum, John 113
Man Mountain Dean 163, 165-166
Mara, Adele 190
Markson, Ben 94
Marsh, Marion 138
Marshall, George 230
Marx Brothers 20, 52, 134, 136
Maxwell, Edwin 12
Mayor of Hell, The 64
McDonald, Frank 175
McHugh, Frank 15, 26, 74, 76, 90, 111
McHugh, Matt 175
Meusel, Bob 100
Miller, Marilyn 6, 8-9
Millican, James 223
Mills Brothers 209
Milton Berle Show 229
Mix, Tom 142
Modern Times 232
Molly and Me 94
Monroe, Marilyn 232, 233

Moore, Dickie 163, 164-165
Munson, Ona 26
Never Say Die 174
Night at the Opera, A 134
Nugent, Edward J. 42
Oakie, Jack 160
Oakland, Vivien 56
On With The Show 4-6
Osborne, Vivienne 186
Painted Faces 5-6
Parsons, Louella 48, 119, 136
Petrified Forest, The 129
Pickford, Mary 113
Pidgeon, Walter 27
Pitts, ZaSu 230
Pollack, Sydney 88
Pollard, Snub 230
Porky in Wackyland 141
Prevost, Frank 2
Price, Vincent 233
Pride of the Marines 175
Puddin' Head 195
Randolf, Anders 17, 18, 21, 24, 28
Raye, Martha 171, 172, 174, 175, 176, 198, 210, 215, 217, 218, 219
Rehg, Wally 100
Reinhart, Max 113
Rice, Florence 146
Rice, Jack 215
Ride Em Cowboy 209
Roach, Hal 62, 74, 160
Roberti, Lyda 160
Roberts, Beverly 123, 168, 169
Robinson, Edward G 41, 185, 186
Robinson, Bill 219
Robinson, Frances 186
Rogers, Ginger 53, 55, 56, 58, 62, 142
Rogers, Roy 192, 195, 207, 215
Rooney, Mickey 98
Rubin, Benny 94
Ruby, Harry 35, 37, 39, 81, 94
Runyon, Damon 77
Sally 6-9
Salute 20
Scatterbrain 195

Schenck, Joe 119
Schilling, Gus 207
Schlesinger, Leon 141
Screen Director's Playhouse 230
Sedgwick, Edward 142
Sennett, Mack 63
Shakespeare, William 98, 104, 110, 111, 112, 113, 114, 115, 116, 145, 212, 213, 214
Show Boat 228
Shuster, Joe 161
Siegel, Jerry 161
Silent Partner, The 230
Skipworth, Alison 158, 159
Some Like it Hot 232-233
Song of the West 9-10
Sons of the Desert 160
Sterling, Ford 9
Strange Love of Molly Louvain 109
Taming of the Shrew 114
They Shoot Horses Don't They 88
Thorpe, Jim 100
Three on a Match 109
Three Stooges 35, 138, 155, 156, 157
Time of their Lives 191
Todd, Mike 231
Todd, Thelma 35, 38, 71, 74, 76
Toler, Sidney. 158, 159
Tourneur, Jacques 233
Travis, June 126, 164
Tucker, Forrest 189
Upson, William Hazlett 124, 126
Urecal, Minerva 202
Verne, Jules 231
Vogan, Emmett 207
Wallis, Hal 96
Warde, Anthony 186
Warner, Jack 120
Waters, Ethel 4
Wellman William 16, 17, 18, 22, 23
Wessell, Dick 186
Westcott, Gordon 84, 89, 94
Wheeler and Woolsey 20, 41, 52
White, Alice 79
White, Marjorie 34-36

Whiting, Jack 12
Whole Town's Talking, The 186
Wilder, Billy 232, 235
Wilson, Charles 125
Woodbury, Joan 190
Woods, Edward 42
Wright, Will 192
Wright, William 201
Wylie, Phillip 163
Wyman, Jane 158, 159
York, Duke 160
Ziegfeld, Florenz 6

www.ingramcontent.com/pod-product-compliance
Lightning Source LLC
Chambersburg PA
CBHW060117170426
43198CB00010B/930